THE DIVINE PERSPECTIVE
ON LIFE, DEATH, AND DAILY LIVING

A Study of the Christian Mindset

JOHN MARINELLI

The Divine Perspective On Life, Death and Daily Living
A Study of The Christian Mindset
Copyright © 2023 John Marinelli
Ocala, Florida …All rights reserved.

First Edition: 8/2023

Print ISBN: 978-1-0882-2990-3
eBook ISBN: 978-1-0882-2992-7

Cover and Formatting: Streetlight Graphics
Contact: johnmarinelli@embarqmail.com

This book is protected under US copyright laws. Any reproduction or other use is prohibited without the written permission of the author.

No part of this book may be reproduced, scanned, or distributed in any printed or electronic form without permission. Please do not participate in or encourage piracy of copyrighted materials in violation of the author's rights. Thank you for respecting the hard work of this author.

TABLE OF CONTENTS

Preface	1
Introduction	3
Chapter One	5
Chapter two	8
Chapter Three	16
Chapter Four	20
Chapter Five	24
Chapter Six	27
Chapter Seven	33
Chapter Eight	37
Chapter Nine	54
Chapter Ten	58
Conclusion	63
About The Author John Marinelli	66
Gallery of Encouraging Christian Poems	67

PREFACE

The "Divine Perspective" is a study of the Christian Mindset and how it effects a person's values and lifestyle. The study addresses the need for Christian believers to examine their values and lifestyle and adjust accordingly to attain a Christian mindset.

The author presents a seven step, walk through the scriptures, opportunity that will help the reader to be renewed and transformed into a mindset that is pleasing unto the Lord. He also presents a gallery of anointed poems for the edification of the soul.

Life, death and daily living were selected as the basis for this study because they best illustrate the essence of man's struggle on earth.

This book is an easy read with lots of Bible support to document the author's teachings.

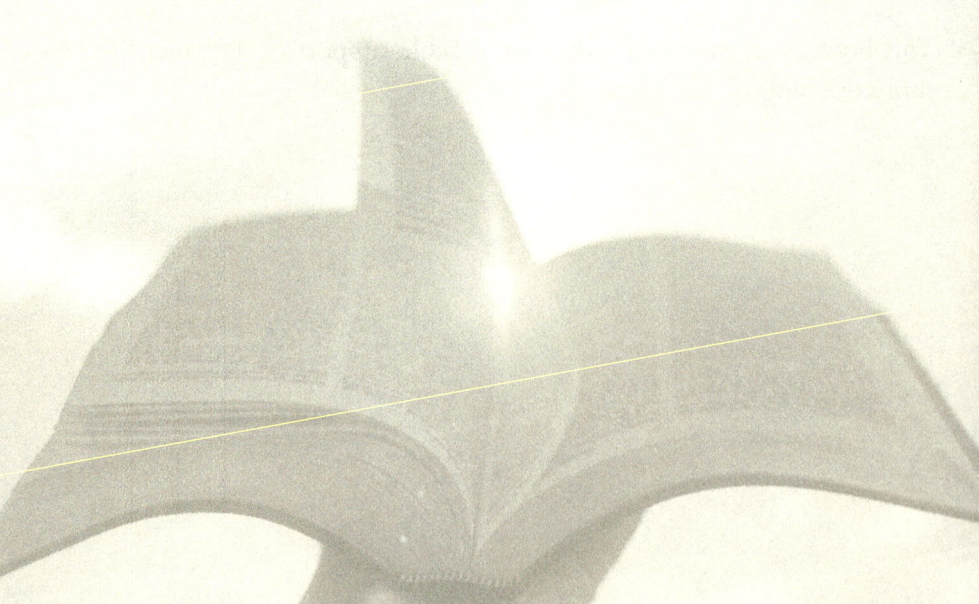

INTRODUCTION

We live in an upside-down world. Today's society calls good evil and evil good. Lies become truth and truth is now seen as right-wing lies. Most folks don't know exactly what to believe.

The word, "Perspective" according to the dictionary, means, a particular attitude toward or way of regarding something; a point of view: We often say, "from the editor's perspective" or "my wife's perspective" and even sometimes say, "from God's perspective." In all cases we are referring to a "Point of View."

God sees things from a certain point of view that is far greater and more insightful than ours. His view on life, death and our daily living is much different than what we see. Our view is marred by sin, confusion and a general lack of understanding.

Jesus saw things in a "Divine Perspective" that was totally different than those around him. You'll remember what he said about faith and the mustard seed. *"for verily I say unto you, If ye have faith as a grain of mustard seed, ye shall say unto this mountain, Remove hence to yonder place; and it shall remove; and nothing shall be impossible unto you."* Matthew 17:20 His perspective was based upon doing the impossible. He actually believed that the impossible was possible if you believed.

His "Divine Perspective" or should I say "Point of View" led him to heal the sick, feed the 5,000 with a little boy's lunch, cast out devils from tormented folks and even raise the dead. His view was not clouded with sin. His Heavenly Father was greater than anything and anyone.

The odd thing about this, "Divine Perspective," is that Jesus told his disciples that they could also experience this type of reality. All they had to do is have faith, not a great amount of faith but a small amount, as little as a mustard seed, which is the smallest of all seeds.

Let's take a deeper look into perspectives and the "Divine Perspective," in particular.

CHAPTER ONE

Our Perspectives Matter

The Bible says that death is an appointment. Here's what the Bible says about that…(And as it is appointed unto men once to die, after this the judgment) Hebrews 9:27 It can be a date far into the future or it can be scheduled for today. Only God knows when death will occur.

Human beings look at death in several ways, based upon their age. When we are young, we look at life as if it will never end. Our perspective is most often fashioned by our ambition to become. We are a, "Want-A-Be" looking to grow and develop into someone of importance. We seek after fame, fortune, power and acceptance. We are the master of our own destiny and rule over every circumstance, at least we try. However, life has a way of throwing us a curve ball and spoiling all of our well-intentioned plans.

As we grow up and attain adulthood, most of us find out that what we wanted cannot be because of education, lack of opportunity or some other roadblock. Others manage to get what they wanted only to find it wasn't what they thought it would be. Then still, there are those that give up along the way, losing their ambition and fall by the wayside, ending up in a menial job and lifestyle that they didn't really want.

It's not what happens to you that defeats you. It is how you perceive it and how you react to it that determines your victory or your defeat. I am sure you have heard about the guy that sees obstacles as steppingstones on the way to glory. Whereas other folks see them as mountains of difficulty and pools of sorrow. I guess you could boil it down to being positive or negative. But it is more than that. Your belief system is what guides your thoughts and influences your decisions. You are what you believe. Here's what the Bible says:

"As a man thinks, in his heart, so is he" Proverbs 23:7 You are what you think, not what you say. That's why we can rarely see the real person. Folks say a lot of things but believe the opposite. When we discover their trickery, we call them "Two-Faced," because they try to hide their real self, showing only what they think we want to see.

If we are to be who we really are, we need to be whatever that persona is… all the time. When we do, we allow Christ to shine in and through our personality. It is not masked with ego, or other faces of evil. Yes, folks will see you at your best and most likely at your worst. However, they will also see Jesus as you surrender all to him as the Lord of your life.

Perspectives really do matter. What you believe about yourself and about God is the basis for living life. It is here that you develop stability, sound minded judgments, rationality and a true sense of reality. What other folks think or say does not matter.

Your perspectives rule the day and governs your actions. If it is in line with the Word of God, you will end up blessed beyond measure, loved without limits and at peace in an upside-down world that is ablaze with the fires of hell.

There are good perspectives and there are bad ones. Remember, a perspective is a point of view. If your point of view is that it is ok to kill unborn babies, I would say that it is a bad perspective, but that is just my opinion. However, we all must give an account to God for the actions we live out in the flesh. We will stand before the throne of God and explain our actions and defend our beliefs.

I believe that a person can hold fast to a perspective that is wrong and live out its consequences, never knowing the truth. They have a free will to do so but they ought to think about what the Bible says first,

"Take heed therefore that the light which is in thee be not darkness." Luke 11:35 We should always look deeply into a matter and judge its redeeming value before accepting it as our own.

I am sure that you know there are many points of view or perspectives in life. We form opinions on lots of different subjects. Abortion is only one. There are also choices to make and decisions to enact on such matters as:

1. Living a moral lifestyle
2. Being truthful or being a Lier
3. Being Straight or Gay
4. Being kind or argumentative
5. Having children or not
6. Getting married or living together without being married
7. Believing that there is a God or being an atheist

We seem to live in a valley of decisions and are forced to select which way we will go. Every choice is a point of view that establishes a perspective. Put them all together and you have a portrait of you. They define who you are and how you feel about certain things in life. They also determine the road you will travel through life whether to heaven or to hell.

God also has perspectives. They all fit into his "Divine Will" If we follow Jesus, we will share in his perspectives or points of view and that will set us apart from the world and its immoral lifestyle. We will be transformed by the renewing of our minds and, like the butterfly, soar to heights never available to us before. The impossible will become possible. We will see the future unfold before our eyes as we move in the Spirit from glory to glory.

CHAPTER TWO

Perspectives Need Feet

Your perspectives must have feet to operate properly. I am sure you have heard that *"Faith Without Works Is Dead."* The phrase is found in the Bible, James 2:17. If someone claims to have faith but does not show it through their actions, then their faith is dead or *useless*. So it is with our belief system.

If I have a perspective (A Belief) that says fornication (sex before marriage) is against God's will, I will need to live in that belief and stand up for it to prove that that I really believe it. If, on the other hand, we engage in immoral sex, our belief (Perspective) is useless. It cannot protect us from violating God's laws and divine will for our lives.

When we hold fast to our confession of faith, we put feet to our perspectives and thus walk circumspectly (Upright) before the Lord and those around us. Our walk must match our talk. If we believe, we walk the walk and talk the talk. This is the true path that leads us to be a witness unto the Lord. It also keeps the devil and all his demons at bay. We eliminate the channel by which evil invades our souls and destroys our peace.

It is important to realize that we are not under any preconceived notion or expectation that requires us to be righteous in order to attain God's grace and salvation. It was while we were lost and dead in our sin that Christ died for us. It was not based upon our right doing or law keeping ability. Ephesians 2:5

The Bible gives us a clear example of a church that Paul said was foolish because they started out with a perspective that was acceptable to God but somehow drifted away from that belief into another that was not acceptable. Here's what he said:

"O foolish Galatians, who hath bewitched you, that ye should not obey the truth, before whose eyes Jesus Christ hath been evidently set forth, crucified among you? This only would I learn of you, Received ye the Spirit by the works of the law, or by the hearing of faith?

Are ye so foolish? having begun in the Spirit, are ye now made perfect by the flesh? Have ye suffered so many things in vain? if it be yet in vain. He therefore that ministers to you the Spirit, and worketh miracles among you, does he it by the works of the law, or by the hearing of faith?

Even as Abraham believed God, and it was accounted to him for righteousness. Know ye therefore that they which are of faith, the same are the children of Abraham. And the scripture, foreseeing that God would justify the heathen through faith, preached before the gospel unto Abraham, saying, In thee shall all nations be blessed.

So then they which be of faith are blessed with faithful Abraham. For as many as are of the works of the law are under the curse: for it is written, cursed is every one that continues not in all things which are written in the book of the law to do them. But that no man is justified by the law in the sight of God, it is evident: for, the just shall live by faith." Galatians 3:1-11

You can see by what Paul is saying, that faith is the motivator that encourages the believer to hold fast to his or her perspective. We cannot shift gears because everybody around us is. If it is true, then it is true and no soft-spoken guy or forward speaking gal with an attitude can draw us away.

A perspective is a way of thinking. A standard is a lifestyle that governs your actions. It is my perspectives that form my belief system. My system of beliefs become standards by-which I live my life. If I believe that being moral is a good thing, I set a standard that dictates my actions from day to day. Some will call this being a Conservative. On the other hand, others will say that being moral is out of date for this time and place and that society demands a more liberal view.

As I mentioned, my standard is based upon my beliefs. This creates a battle between conservatives and liberals that is acted out in society. Right now, immorality is winning because the hearts of men and women have turned away from the truth of the Bible and God's ultimate will.

The real issue is "Absolute" truth. The Bible teaches that God's will is to be righteous which includes being moral. This is presented as an absolute. However, the liberal thinker denies the concept of "Absolute" and says everything is relative and thus subject to the situation. They will say that Christians set the bar or standard too high. The Christian, however, holds fast to a Godly standard, even if it is impossible to attain or sustain.

Just because I cannot be holy and often fall short of the standard that God has set in place, doesn't mean or even suggest that the standard is flawed. It only shows me that I have fallen short of being what God wanted me to be. It also shows that I am indeed in need of a Savior that will redeem me from, not only the curse of the law (or Standard) but also the sin that dwells within my heart that keeps me from being holy or righteous.

Here's what AllAboutPhilosophy.org says about absolute truth

"Absolute Truth" is defined as inflexible reality: fixed, invariable, unalterable facts. For example, it is a fixed, invariable, unalterable fact that there are absolutely no square circles and there are absolutely no round squares. You can't logically argue against the existence of absolute truth. To argue against something is to establish that a truth exists.

You cannot argue against absolute truth unless an absolute truth is the basis of your argument. Consider a few of the classic arguments and declarations made by those who seek to argue against the existence of absolute truth… "There are no absolutes."

First of all, the relativist is declaring there are absolutely no absolutes. That is an absolute statement. The statement is logically contradictory. If the statement is true, there is, in fact, an absolute - there are absolutely no absolutes. "Truth Is Relative."

Again, this is an absolute statement implying truth is absolutely relative. Besides positioning an absolute, suppose the statement was true and "truth is relative. Everything including that statement would be relative. If a statement is relative, it is not always true. If "truth is relative" it is not always true, sometimes truth is not relative.

This means there are absolutes, which means the above statement is false. When you follow the logic, relativist arguments will always contradict themselves.

The liberal point of view will say, "Who Knows What The Truth Is, Right?"

In the same sentence the speaker declares that no one knows what the truth is, then he turns around and asks those who are listening to affirm the truth of his statement. "No One Knows What The Truth Is."

The speaker obviously believes his statement is true. There are philosophers who actually spend countless hours toiling over thick volumes written on the "meaninglessness" of everything. We can assume they think the text is meaningful!

Then there are those philosophy teachers, who teach their students:

1. "No one's opinion is superior to anyone else's.
2. There is no hierarchy of truth or values.
3. Anyone's viewpoint is just as valid as anyone else's viewpoint.
4. We all have our own truth." Then they turn around and grade the papers

Absolute Truth And Morality Demand Standards

Morality is a facet of absolute truth. Thus, relativists often declare, "It's wrong for you to impose your morals on me." By declaring something is wrong, the relativist is contradicting himself by imposing his morals upon you. You might hear, "There is no right, there is no wrong!" You must ask, is that statement right or wrong?

If you catch a relativist in the act of doing something they know is absolutely wrong, and you try to point it out to them, they may respond in anger, "Truth is relative!

There's no right and there's no wrong! We should be able to do whatever we want!" If that is a true statement and there is no right and there is no wrong, and everyone should be able to do whatever they want, then why have they become angry? What basis do they have for their anger? You can't be appalled by an injustice, or anything else for that matter, unless an absolute has somehow been violated.

Whatever Happened To The Truth?

Here's what Linda Keffer of Focus On The Family Has To Say

In our world today, the idea of ultimate truth — something that is true at all times in all places and has relevance for our lives — is about as extinct as the dinosaur.

In fact, nearly three out of four Americans say there is no such thing as ultimate, or absolute, truth. And the numbers don't look much better among those who claim to follow Jesus.

In a society where ultimate truth is treated like a fairy tale, an outdated idea or even an insult to human intelligence, the motto of the day becomes, "WHATEVER!" Believe whatever you want. Do whatever seems best to you. Live for whatever brings you pleasure, as long as it doesn't hurt anyone. And of course, be tolerant. Don't try to tell anyone that their "whatever" is wrong. But where does that leave us?

If we have ultimate truth, it gives us both a way to explain the world around us and a basis for making decisions. Without it, we're alone. We're just 7 billion organisms running around, bumping into each other with nothing unifying to work for or believe in. It's every man for himself. And we're without a purpose; if there's no true story of where we came from and why we're here, then there's nothing that really gives our lives meaning. Sounds a little depressing, huh? And maybe frightening. Has life always been like this?

Do we have to carry on this way? No! In fact, in the scope of history, *"whatever"* is a pretty new way of viewing the world.

Living In A *"Whatever"* World

If there is no basis for moral decisions, then whatever you choose to do is fine. Of course, most people like to believe that they have some basis for the decisions they make. So, we've constructed our own standards:

- **Science & Reason** Even though most people have thrown out reason as the source of ultimate truth, some still cling to it. "If I can't see it, hear it, smell it, taste it, touch it and test it, it can't be true," they say.
- **Popular Opinion** You only have to look as far as your TV to know that society thinks popular opinion is a good basis for making decisions. Otherwise, why would our advertisements tell us to "catch the wave" or make the "choice of a new generation"? All these ads appeal to the idea that "everyone is doing it" and that you should, too.
- **Feelings & Emotions** are perhaps the most popular basis for making choices today. After all, how can anyone argue with how you feel? If feelings are a good standard for decision-making, then you'll never have to come up with a better defense than, "I did it because I felt like it."

It doesn't take a lot of "what if" scenarios to realize that there are major problems with all these approaches to decision-making. What if you're asking a question that science can't answer? What if the group changes its opinion? How do you know which one was right? and what if following your feelings leads you to an action with consequences you can't handle? We've gotten ourselves into this "whatever" mess, but it's getting harder and harder to live here. So how do we get out?

The first rung on the ladder out of this "no-truth" hole is realizing that it's reasonable to desire truth. In fact, those who tell you it's useless or narrowminded to believe in ultimate truth have more explaining to do than they can pull off.

When someone says, "There is no such thing as absolute truth," that person is actually making a statement that he or she believes to be absolutely true.

Contradictory, isn't it? And it's even reasonable to search for ultimate truth in God. Those who say there is no God on whom to base our standards have a very hard time dealing with these questions:

- Why do we have personalities? If there is no personal God who "shared these bits of His personality with us," where did we get them?
- Why do the pieces of the universe fit together so intricately? If there isn't a higher standard outside the natural world ordering the way things work, then why do they work so well?
- Why do we have a strong desire for purpose and meaning in life? If there is no "big picture" that explains where we came from and why we're here, why do we ask questions about purpose and spend our lives trying to find the answers? These questions don't automatically take us to the truth, but they do give us a place to start looking.

Is there any evidence for the existence of absolute truth? Yes, there is.

First, there is the human conscience, that certain "something" within us that tells us the world should be a certain way, that some things are right and some are wrong. Our conscience convinces us there is something wrong with suffering, starvation, rape, pain, and evil, and it makes us aware that love, generosity, compassion, and peace are positive things for which we should strive. This is universally true in all cultures in all times.

The Bible describes the role of the human conscience in Romans 2:14-16: "Indeed, when Gentiles, who do not have the law, do by nature things required by the law, they are a law for themselves, even though they do not have the law, since they show that the requirements of the law are written on their hearts, their consciences also bearing witness, and their thoughts now accusing, now even defending them. This will take place on the day when God will judge men's secrets through Jesus Christ, as my gospel declares."

The *second* evidence for the existence of absolute truth is science. Science is simply the pursuit of knowledge, the study of what we know and the quest to know more. Therefore, all scientific study must, by necessity, be founded upon the belief that there are objective realities existing in the world and these realities can be discovered and proven. Without absolutes, what would there be to study? How could one know that the findings of science are real? In fact, the very laws of science are founded on the existence of absolute truth.

The *third* evidence for the existence of absolute or universal truth is religion. All the religions of the world attempt to give meaning and definition to life. They are born out of mankind's desire for something more than simple existence. Through religion, humans seek God, hope for the future, forgiveness of sins, peace in the midst of struggle, and answers to our deepest questions.

Religion is really evidence that mankind is more than just a highly evolved animal. It is evidence of a higher purpose and of the existence of a personal and purposeful Creator who implanted in man the desire to know him. And if there is indeed a Creator, then he becomes the standard for absolute truth, and it is his authority that establishes that truth. Fortunately, there is such a Creator, and he has revealed his truth to us through his Word, the Bible.

Knowing absolute or universal truth is only possible through a personal relationship with the One who claims to be the Truth—Jesus Christ.

Jesus claimed to be the only way, the only truth, the only life and the only path to God (John 14:6). The fact that absolute truth does exist points us to the truth that there is a sovereign God who created the heavens and the earth and who has revealed himself to us in order that we might know him personally through his Son Jesus Christ. That is the absolute truth.

Our standards need to be based upon "Absolute Truth" and that can only be found in the Word of God.

CHAPTER THREE

Perspectives Foster Rejection

Have you ever been rejected by someone? Jesus said, (John 15:18-25)

"If the world hates you, keep in mind that it hated me first. If you belonged to the world, it would love you as its own. As it is, you do not belong to the world, but I have chosen you out of the world. That is why the world hates you. Remember what I told you: 'A servant is not greater than his master.' If they persecuted me, they will persecute you also. If they obeyed my teaching, they will obey yours also.

They will treat you this way because of my name, for they do not know the one who sent me. If I had not come and spoken to them, they would not be guilty of sin; but now they have no excuse for their sin. Whoever hates me hates my Father as well. If I had not done among them the works no one else did, they would not be guilty of sin. As it is, they have seen, and yet they have hated both me and my Father. But this is to fulfill what is written in their Law: They hated me without reason."

Rejection is a large part of why we feel bad, experience low self-esteem, suffer under depression and anxiety and withdraw from life. Why don't they like me? I never did anything to hurt them. We constantly ask ourselves "Why" and yet never get an answer.

Rejection Is Not A Measurement of True Worth

God sees us differently than we see ourselves. We often condemn ourselves because of our actions that, in our own eyes, are not righteous. They fall short of God's standard. Thus, we feel bad and even emotionally punish ourselves. That is because we do not understand the true nature of God and his marvelous grace.

Then there are the well-meaning critical acquaintances that feel they know best how you should be and act. These are the folks that put expectations on you that are no more than judgmental fiery darts from hell. Avoid them at all cost.

News Flash! God is Love. Yes, he hates the rebellious wicked soul that seeks to overthrow him and his kingdom. However, the repentant soul in not despised. God's hand of forgiveness and fellowship is always stretched out with compassion and blessings.

Well Jesus tells us why we are being rejected. He answered that question in the gospel of John. The "They" people Jesus refers to are those that do not obey his teachings. Think about it! These folks will not acknowledge Jesus as the only begotten Son of God and will not follow him. It only makes sense that they will not acknowledge you or listen to you. They do not like your standards, (way of life) and how you reflect the glory of God. Your Point of View is not theirs. They really feel that you are wrong, not them. The light in them is actually darkness.

Stop trying to figure out why you are rejected. It could be because you are too pretty, too educated, too tall, too rich or too poor. Just know that it is because you are a Christian that loves the Lord and seeks to obey his teachings.

The devil will try to keep you in a continuous loop of confusion and frustration as you try to find out why. Now you know why so go on with what God has for you.

Remember, God has not rejected you. You are now the righteousness of God in Christ Jesus. (*For he made him who knew no sin to be sin for us, that we might become the righteousness of God in him.*) 2 Corinthians 5:21

The best way to deal with rejection is to know who you are in Christ. If you know your rights as a child of God, you can use that knowledge to cast down every anti-Christ thought or attack against you, even rejection. Hear what the apostle Paul said to the church of the 1st century.

"for the weapons of our warfare are not carnal, but mighty through God to the pulling down of strong holds;) casting down imaginations, and every high thing that exalts itself against the knowledge of God, and bringing into captivity every thought to the obedience of Christ; and having in a readiness to revenge all disobedience, when your obedience is fulfilled." 2 Corinthians 10:4-7

Most of us don't see ourselves as warriors in Christ. However, as the old hymn says, "Onward Christian Soldiers, marching as to war." We must, at all cost, reject the rejection, because it comes from the devil through the person that tosses the zinger.

Notice that your obedience to the revealed or known will of God must be fulfilled. It is only then that we can bring every thought or action into captivity. It is only then that we can cast it down and watch it fizzle before us.

If you can see spiritually, you will see evil spirits flinging fiery darts at you in the form of criticism, accusations and half-truths. Your position, as a "Born Again" believer, gives you power over demons, sickness and especially those that reject you.

Another way to deal with rejection is to realize that you are washed in the blood of Jesus and have been cleansed from all sin. Forever... Again, hear what the apostle John said.

"But if we walk in the light, as he is in the light, we have fellowship one with another, and the blood of Jesus Christ his Son cleanses us from all sin. If we say that we have no sin, we deceive ourselves, and the truth is not in us.

If we confess our sins, he is faithful and just to forgive us our sins, and to cleanse us from all unrighteousness. I John 1:7-9

The power of verse nine above is that God is faithful to forgive and continually cleanse. That is what the Greek text implies. It is a continual process because we are habitual sinners…even after we are saved…so we confess and he forgives.

It is important to realize that most of the time we don't know when we are committing an act of sin. It comes natural to us. It is in our nature to sin. It is part of our personality. The Bible calls this, "The Deeds of the flesh." Galatians 5-22.

God wants us to be holy but knows we cannot achieve that standard. That is why he sent his only begotten Son, Jesus, to Calvary's cross, to pay the penalty for our sin so we might be free to serve him. Knowing this and believing it empowers us to overcome the criticisms of others. One last scripture:

"Moreover, whom he did predestinate, them he also called: and whom he called, them he also justified: and whom he justified, them he also glorified. What shall we then say to these things? If God be for us, who can be against us? He that spared not his own Son, but delivered him up for us all, how shall he not with him also freely give us all things? Who shall lay anything to the charge of God's elect? It is God that justifies.

Who is he that condemns? It is Christ that died, yea rather, that is risen again, who is even at the right hand of God, who also makes intercession for us. Who shall separate us from the love of Christ? Shall tribulation, or distress, or persecution, or famine, or nakedness, or peril, or sword?

As it is written, for thy sake we are killed all the day long; we are accounted as sheep for the slaughter. Nay, in all these things we are more than conquerors through him that loved us. For I am persuaded, that neither death, nor life, nor angels, nor principalities, nor powers, nor things present, nor things to come, nor height, nor depth, nor any other creature, shall be able to separate us from the love of God, which is in Christ Jesus our Lord." Romans 8:30-39

The next time you feel rejected, laugh in its face and remember that you are accepted in the beloved. Ephesians 1:6 If you need to, rehearse all the Bible truths that support you being accepted. Look these up and you will get blessed beyond measure:

John 3:16, Ephesians 1:6, Romans 5:8, Romans 5:17-19, Romans 8:31, I John 1:9, Ephesians 1:5 and lots more awaiting your research.

CHAPTER FOUR

Perspectives Require Choices

Perspectives do not grow on trees. They are a series of individual choices on a variety of subjects. They are usually issue related and most likely popular with modern day thought. Here's a list of today's modern-day thoughts:

Gay Rights; Transvestites; Sex Before Marriage; Polygamy; Alcohol; Drugs; Violence; Religion; Politically Correct; Pornography; Human Trafficking; Child & Spouse and Animal Abuse; Abortion; Gun Control…and so on.

I could go on with the list but the above will do to make my point. We have to decide on all of these issues and more. There is no escape. How we believe will shape our outlook on life, who we hang out with and what type of person we actually are. There is no middle ground. If we decide not to take sides, we vote for the evil. Jesus said this to his disciples, "If you are not for me, you are against me" Matthew 12:30

"Who are you?" Or should I say, "Who do you want to be?" The choice is yours. However, realize that you are setting a standard for each issue. Combine them and you will create a lifestyle. The lifestyle you create can be and is often labeled Conservative or Liberal; Godly or Ungodly; Good or Evil; Democrat or Republican.

I've said it before, "Humanity lives in the valley of decisions. Each decision creates a standard that becomes your point of view." Our perspective requires a choice or many choices. We must decide what our life will be like. God has given me a "Free Will" to do anything I want. I can choose to be a drunk, an astronaut, a butcher, baker and even a candle stick maker. My life is the sum total of my choices.

As Christians, we want to make Jesus Lord over our everyday and seek him for divine revelation, wisdom and discernment so we can operate within his will. It is his will that brings us blessings, spiritual growth, true fellowship and acceptance. We find ourselves in him and can look ahead into eternity. It is the only way to realize our God-given destiny.

The question may arise, "How do I know that I am making the right choice?" I can answer that by saying 1st of all…

"And let the peace of God rule in your hearts, to the which also ye are called in one body; and be ye thankful." Colossians 3:15

If the peace of God is to rule, you will need to be sure you have surrendered your will to Jesus so his Holy Spirit can fill you with the fruit of the Spirit. Then you will gain access to the peace of God. See Galatians 5:22 for a list of the fruit. When you are filled, you get it all.

God's peace will rule. The implication is to referee as in a game of football. If a player gets off sides or does something that is against the established rules, he will blow his whistle and cry out, naming the penalty. The Holy Spirit should be considered your personal referee. He will call out the penalty by taking your peace. If you notice that his peace is no longer in control, you are "Off Sides."

The request is to allow the peace of God to referee your life thereby directing your path through this world.

Another way of knowing you are making the right choices in life is to base them on the revealed Word of God. Did you know that there are over 3,000 promises of God and many direct teachings on the will of God and how man should respond?

The Bible is full of "Absolute Truths." You can use them as a foundation for your perspectives. They can and should become your personal point of view. Let's look at one so you get the point.

"Thou shalt not commit adultery." Because this directive was given to man by God, it is an absolute which means, it cannot be altered due to situation, personal clout, or even legislative decree. Adultery is wrong because

God said so…end of story…no debate. However, the reason it is wrong is because marriage reflects God's relationship with man and adultery breaks that bond and dishonors him.

If I set my standard on this issue to match what I see in the scriptures, I create a perspective that will guide me through life and keep me from any future temptation. Plus, I have aligned myself to the obedience of Christ and now am prepared to cast down imaginations and every thought that sets itself up above the knowledge of God.

There is one other way to know that you are making the right choice. It is to discuss the options and possibilities with a trusted friend or group of friends. However, beware that you are selecting friends that are really friends. Even Jesus had a devil in his circle of trusted disciples. I share this option because of what I see in the scriptures. Check out this one…

"For by wise counsel, thou shalt make thy war: and in a multitude of counsellers there is safety." Proverbs 24:6

Seeking wise counsel leads to a safe decision that brings peace to the soul. Wise counsel can have ideas and options you never thought of. Just know that wisdom is the ability to understand what the knowledge brings. Your Christian counselor friends must have a good handle on what the scriptures say. They need to be well versed in Bible truth.

One more thing…listen to hear the voice of God. He will speak to your heart through an unction, feeling, dream or Biblical revelation as you read the scriptures. Here are a few scriptures to validate this action:

Isiah 30:21- "And thine ears shall hear a word behind thee, saying, this is the way, walk ye in it, when ye turn… And thine ears shall hear a word behind thee, saying, this is the way, walk ye in it, when ye turn to the right hand, and when ye turn to the left."

John 8:47- "He that is of God, heareth God's words, ye therefore hear them not because ye are not of God."

John 10:27-30 – "My sheep hear my voice, and I know them, and they follow me: And I give unto them eternal life; and they shall never perish, neither shall any man pluck them out of my hand. My Father, which gave them me, is greater than all; and no man is able to pluck them out of my Father's hand. I and my Father are one."

Romans 8:16 – "The Spirit itself bears witness with our spirit, that we are the children of God:"

Note: If the Spirit of God bears witness with our spirit, then he is talking to us all the time. After all, he is our counselor, guide and seal unto the day of our redemption. We are communicating all the time with God through his Spirit. Surely, he will help us to make the right choices in life. We just need to listen.

Why not spend some time reading the Bible and praying. You may discover that God is talking to you and the Holy Spirit is leading you to a divine revelation.

CHAPTER FIVE

Perspective Build Roadways

The perspectives we choose lead us into life or death. The Godly choices lead to God and his eternal kingdom. The ungodly choice will lead us into sorrow, suffering, regret, unhappiness and ultimately eternal death.

Here's a revelation. We speak out what we believe. Our tongue flaps in the wind, causing life or death to invade our souls. We are even held accountable by God for every idle word. Matthew 12:26

If we speak lies, we become a liar and after a while begin to live out those lies. Say it enough times and you own it. On the other hand, speak the truth and you will begin to walk in it and become a truthful person. The truth will set you free. Here's what Jesus said as recorded by the apostle John:

"And ye shall know the truth, and the truth shall make you free." John 8:32

Jesus also said, about the devil when speaking to some of the religious leaders, "ye are of your father the devil, and the lusts of your father ye will do. He was a murderer from the beginning, and abode not in the truth, because there is no truth in him. When he speaks a lie, he speaks of his own: for he is a liar, and the father of it." John 8:44

What road are you on? If you are not sure, listen to yourself, not when you are around other folks but when you are all alone, in the quiet of your own heart, in the thought life of your soul. That is where you can examine your deeds done in the flesh to see if they measure up to the standard God has established. If you find that you are on a road that leads you to the fires of hell, repent and ask to be cleansed with the blood of Jesus. I John 1:9

Do you remember the commencement speech at your high school graduation?" I can remember it well and it's been over 60 years ago. The speaker asked us one question. He said, "Where do you think you will be 10 years from now?" Then he said, "Take your time and consider it carefully because one day you will look back and remember your answer."

There are companies that do research on how certain classes end up. I read one a few years ago that revealed some shocking statistics. None of the senior class thought they would be dead; however, many died within that time period. Others became drug addicts, criminals and a large percent of the class were divorced and remarried. Unfortunately, more children than we think grow up in single parent homes.

All of these destinations listed above are a result of poor choices and/or bad decision making. I speak for myself first. You can jump in where ever you fit. I do not say that everyone did poorly. Many went on to have very rewarding and productive lives.

The point I want to make is that each one of us, from graduation until now, took a certain path. They walked a road in life that led them to the destination they are now. It just didn't happen overnight or with a flash of magic. We make choices that establish perspectives that create our point of view on lots of issues that guides us to our final destination. It just doesn't happen on its own. Here's what Jesus said:

"Jesus said, "Whatever you want men to do to you, do also to them." Immediately after giving this Golden Rule, he said in verses 13 and 14,

"Enter by the narrow gate; for wide is the gate and broad is the way that leads to destruction, and there are many who go in by it. Because narrow is the gate and difficult [restricted] is the way which leads to life, and there are few who find it." Matthew 7:12-14

This is a surprising answer because Jesus attached the roads to the way a person lives. The Golden Rule is offered by Jesus to the crowd as a way of life, a perspective that they can use to walk through this world on the way to their final destination.

As I look back over the years since high school, I have seen times where I made foolish choices and based my decisions on greed or some other selfish desire.

Well, what can I say? Only this. "It is never too late to start over in your walk through this world. God will help you to go back to the gates that open up into the paths where folks walk. Just be sure to take the one that opens to the narrow pathway. Starting over is not so bad. Actually, it's sort of fun. It's like getting a second chance at life but now, hopefully, you won't make all the same bad choices you did when you were younger.

We can change our minds and perspective. After all, they are only points of view that we can change at any time. Try it now, depending upon the Lord to guide you every step of the way. He knows the beginning and the end and can easily share them with you. Before you decide, ask the Lord to tell or show you what way or choice is best for you. He will answer you.

CHAPTER SIX

Perspectives Create "Mindsets"

We need to learn how to be transformed from a life of carnality, where sadness, depression and immorality reign. This study, if done seriously, will transform the mind into an abundance of life where love, joy, peace and other attributes of God flow freely. We will be looking at Romans chapter twelve with a look back at the end of chapter eleven. I will also add other supporting scriptures that are relevant to my discussion.

Based on the material from Acts and the Corinthian epistles, the book of Romans clearly indicates that it was written from Corinth on Paul's third missionary journey. Paul had never visited Rome; but after fulfilling his mission of mercy to Jerusalem, he hoped to go to Rome in route to Spain (Rom. 15:23-25). At any rate, the date of the book is probably 60 A.D.

At the end of chapter eleven, Paul says this, "For of him, and through him and to him, are all things: to whom be glory forever. Amen."

The beginning of chapter twelve, Paul continues with a, "Therefore" saying this, "I beseech you *therefore*, brethren, by the mercies of God, that ye present your bodies a living sacrifice, holy, acceptable unto God, which is your reasonable service and be not conformed to this world: but be ye transformed by the renewing of your mind, that ye may prove what is that good, and acceptable, and perfect, will of God."

Romans 12:2 The reason or need for us to be transformed is so we can prove what is that good, and acceptable, and perfect, will of God. Proving or knowing the perfect will of God is discernable but not by worldly methods. It takes the Spirit of God to see into spiritual things. That's why Paul begs us to be transformed.

Paul is begging (Beseeching) the Christians at Rome, on the basis of 11:36, (Because all things are of him, through him and to him, we, 12:1 Therefore, we, by the mercies of God, ought to present our bodies as a living sacrifice which is holy and acceptable unto God.

This action, although noteworthy, is not easy. Paul knew this and thus tells his believers that it will require a transformation from worldly to spiritual; from walking in darkness to walking in the light of God's love; from immorality to morality. Life, as they knew it, would have to radically change.

Their thinking will have to become brand new. The mind will have to be renewed. This is the only way they can be transformed. So…in order to be transformed, we need to exchange our corrupt minds with the mind of Christ. We need to restore our minds to a condition of holiness. The problem is, we've never been in that holy mindset so restoration is seemingly impossible because we don't know what that looks like…or do we?

Most folks, in our current society, are not interested in a new mindset that will deprive them of their current lifestyle. They are perfectly happy being who they are. They like the power to be their own god. Their motto is, "It's my life and I will do it my way."

That is all well and good until life throws you a curve ball and you get laid off from work and end up in a line to get food stamps or government cheese. All is fine until we are hit with cancer, Parkinson disease or something worse. We're doing ok until our spouse runs off with another and leaves us high and dry to take care of the kids.

Here's another *News Flash!* Most of life is beyond our control. We can rule over some of it but not all. We are not God. We can, however, be his child and enjoy his blessings. We just need a mindset to hold on to. Our perspectives create the mindset that forms our point of view in life that fosters faith and leads to God's provisions and blessings.

Renewing our minds will transform us from walking in darkness to the glory of God's love and grace. It will make him Lord and put us under his eternal care.

It seems to me that we have lost our perspectives in life. I just saw on the news how the good old USA is slowly being politically polarized. The conservative voters are moving to "Red" states while the liberals are moving to "Blue" states. The commentator said that it was obvious that the folks that are moving are doing so because they want their kids to grow up with like-minded people and not have to be subjected to ridicule from liberal influences or conservative influences depending on who is moving where. It is not wrong to want to be around folks that think like you. In the same way, Christians tend to gather with other Christians of like mind.

Everyone has a different mindset and walks a different path in life. God wants us all to be of one mind. His destiny is to dwell in all of us with a free hand to rule this world. Our values have a lot to do with how we live our daily lives. However, values come from perspectives that build mindsets that guide us through good and bad times…and the best advantage is that it unifies us so we are one body.

Right now, the devil is fighting against us so we do not capture this truth and apply it. But the time will come when God's children will be one and Jesus will be glorified here on earth. Here's what the Bible says about what we, as believers, should do:

"Let this mind be in you, which was also in Christ Jesus: Who, being in the form of God, thought it not robbery to be equal with God: But made himself of no reputation, and took upon him the form of a servant, and was made in the likeness of men:

And being found in fashion as a man, he humbled himself, and became obedient unto death, even the death of the cross. Wherefore God also hath highly exalted him, and given him a name which is above every name: That at the name of Jesus every knee should bow, of things in heaven, and things in earth, and things under the earth; And that every tongue should confess that Jesus Christ is Lord, to the glory of God the Father." Philippians 2:5-11

Can you see how this is the mindset that Jesus had? He was to condescend from being God to take on the role of a servant. He needed to become obedient even unto the point of death, first to his own will and then the death of the cross.

We are asked to allow this example, accept the same mindset that was in Jesus, a mind of humility. In other words, we are to get over ourselves with all the I & Me selfishness and serve the Lord. The reason is so Jesus can be glorified in us.

You'll remember that Jesus said this about that to the crowd that followed him. He said, "And he said to them all, if any man will come after me, let him deny himself, and take up his cross daily, and follow me." Luke 9:23

Following Jesus was no laughing matter. It was not supposed to be a walk in the park. Followers were to make a life commitment and take on a lifelong mindset to deny themselves and become disciples of Christ. This perspective is divine. It is the "Divine Perspective" that makes us an overcomer in this crazy world.

According to Stanford psychologist Carol Dweck, your beliefs play a pivotal role in what you want and whether you achieve it. She goes on to say that our mindset is a set of beliefs that shape how we make sense of the world and ourselves. It influences how you think, feel, and behave in any given situation. It means that what you believe about yourself impacts your success or failure. Excerpts from Very well Mind Sept. 2022

I've said it before. Your thoughts define you as a person. "For as he thinketh in his heart, so is he:" Proverbs 23:7 So, a penny for your thoughts.

During the 1st century when evil was rampant and Christianity was young, the apostle Paul encouraged the church by saying, "Finally, brethren, whatsoever things are true, whatsoever things *are* honest, whatsoever things *are* just, whatsoever things *are* pure, whatsoever things *are* lovely, whatsoever things *are* of good report; if *there be* any virtue, and if *there be* any praise, think on these things." Philippians 4:8

Paul knew that if the church could shift gears from a negative to a positive view point, they would get through all the persecution and hostility being forced upon them. His answer was to shift their focus onto better things.

The lesson learned for us as Christians who also face hostile voices, criticism and all out rejection is to enact an, "I don't give a flip" attitude towards those that reject us and turn our attention towards those things that are pure, of good report and positive.

There are a lot of folks that have a damaged mindset. They, as a child, were abused or criticized in some way by family, peers or neighbors. They end up insecure or have a low self-esteem. The remedy is, as we discussed already, be transformed by the renewing of your mind. Create the new you based upon Biblical truth and revelation. The easy way is to make a check list of your mindsets. Ask yourself, "What do I think about. Here are a few to add to your list:

God, following Jesus, the social issues of the day like abortion, gay rights, sex before marriage, taking drugs, and so on. If you do not have an opinion, make one and lock it in as your mindset. Be sure to check them against the scriptures to be sure they do not go against God's Word.

The devil will seek to deceive you as you establish or change mindsets. Know that you can change your mind but never, ever move away from what the Bible says.

Do as the apostle Peter instructed us to do. He said, "Be sober, be vigilant; because your adversary the devil, as a roaring lion, walketh about, seeking whom he may devour:" whom resist steadfast in the faith, knowing that the same afflictions are accomplished in your brethren that are in the world. But the God of all grace, who hath called us unto his eternal glory by Christ Jesus, after that ye have suffered a while, make you perfect, stablish, strengthen, settle you." I Peter 5:8-10

The interesting thing about this scripture is that this lion can roar but has no power to hurt you. He cannot violate your free will or cast evil upon you. He has to steal your authority and kill your ability to stand against him. That's why he roars…to frighten you into submission. Paul says to resist him in the faith.

Resisting in the faith is to declare that Jesus is Lord and that he overcame the devil on the cross. His death and resurrection spoiled Satan's kingdom. To resist is not to wage all-out war. It is rather to stand in the knowledge that Jesus has already won the battle and to laugh at the roaring lion, telling him to go away, in the name of Jesus. This is the mindset that keeps us free and away from snares and traps that evil forces set for us. ("When he had disarmed the rulers and authorities, those supernatural forces of evil operating against us, he made a public example of them, exhibiting them as captives in his triumphal procession, having triumphed over them through the cross.") Colossians 2:14-16 Amplified Bible Version.

Mindset is everything. What you believe and what you establish as your value system really does matter.

CHAPTER SEVEN

Perspectives Enable Discernment

The unsaved man is like Adam after he fell from God's grace. He is without God's indwelling Spirit (Breath of Life). He was separated from God and left to walk in spiritual darkness.

The saved man is like Jesus. He possesses the indwelling Spirit of the living God. He is privileged to hear God's voice, understand his logic and be blessed by his wisdom. All of this came to man when he was "Born Again." John 3:16.

The invisible nature of God now shines in and through his children who have been "Born Anew" by his Spirit. It's like a butterfly that once was a crawling worm-like creature that experiences transformation and becomes a beautiful butterfly. This is a vivid picture of a, "New Creature". The old passed away, rather…was transformed into something entirely new.

We are buried into baptism with Christ and raised with him in newness of life. Colossians 2:12 . Anyone who says they are alive in God and does not believe in the burial by baptism and a personal resurrection with Christ is deceived and probably not really saved.

Here's what Paul said to the Galatians: (Chapter Three)

"O foolish Galatians, who hath bewitched you, that ye should not obey the truth, before whose eyes Jesus Christ hath been evidently set forth, crucified among you? This only would I learn of you, Received ye the Spirit by the works of the law, or by the hearing of faith? Are ye so foolish? having begun in the Spirit, are ye now made perfect by the flesh?" Galatians 3:1-35

This is a prime example of a need to be renewed. They drifted away from spiritual things returning to the things of the flesh. If you read on, you will discover that they had abandoned the concept of God's saving grace to trust in the Law of Moses as a spiritual guide for salvation. Paul said they were foolish.

So…we now know that we are to be transformed and the way to accomplish that transformation is to renew our minds…to go back to the simplicity of the gospel and follow in the footsteps of Christ. Let me explain.

The world system of things… like Liberalism, Secularism, Gay Rights, Gender Reclassification and other immoral posturing has worn off on us.

The world's influence has led to a general lack of faith and a great falling away from the gospel of grace. They were once dedicated to God's will, not what society said. He was the center of their life and they found themselves in him, not this world. His mindset was what they sought and found in his lordship. They could see life from his perspective.

However, now they cannot see through the eyes of the Spirit so they revert to religion to sustain them. The problem with religion is that it does not set anyone free. Instead, it puts them in bondage to the laws of that group. The Bible tells us that the Law of Moses, that the Galatians followed, was in fact a school master to show us the need for a Savior. Hear the explanation that Paul gave:

"Wherefore, the law was our schoolmaster to bring us unto Christ, that we might be justified by faith. But after that faith is come, we are no longer under a schoolmaster. For ye are all the children of God by faith in Christ Jesus." Galatians 3:24-26

It was obvious that the church did not understand the concept of Grace. It is defined as, "Unmerited Favor." That means we did not earn it or even deserve it but nevertheless are given it as an act of love by God.

If there were anything we could do it would be to accept it by faith. Keeping a set of rules and regulations cannot get us into heaven. The apostle, John sets the record straight by quoting what Jesus said. Jesus said, *"For God so loved the world, that he gave his only begotten Son, that whosoever believeth in him should not perish, but have everlasting life."* John 3:16

I can remember when I would open the Bible and try to read it, I just found it really hard to understand. Then I read John 3:16 and saw that God loved me and Jesus came to die for my sins and I could have eternal life by believing on him as my personal savior.

I began to accept this as a fact and set it as a perspective that formed a mindset in my thinking and a standard by which I began to live. My point of view slowly became Christian. After that one experience I began to see things in the scriptures. Bible truth began to jump off the page and I began to understand. I had eyes to see and ears to hear and so I listened and discovered my destiny in him.

Your perspectives can and does bring discernment. Life, itself, takes on an entirely new dimension.

Discernment is defined as, "the ability to judge well:" That is to say that you can not only understand but can judge its worth and value in a live situation.

(in Christian contexts) discernment is seen as…perception in the absence of judgment with a view to obtaining spiritual guidance and understanding: This means that your perception of the situation becomes clear as you seek guidance.

The Bible says, "A prudent man foresees the evil, and hides himself; but the simple pass on, and are punished." Proverbs 27:12

A prudent man is a wise man. His wisdom comes from his perspectives. They teach him to not take life at face value but rather to look into the situation to be sure it is ok to proceed. The simple refers to the foolish who continue without looking for danger and are punished. Proverbs 22:3

With all the decisions we face in this life and all the evil traps and deceptions around us, it is good to know that God will give us his wisdom so we can avoid danger and move on in our journey to life eternal.

Our perspectives enable Godly discernment. If you do not have this vital tool, ask the Lord for it and he will give it to you. "If any of you lack wisdom, let him ask of God, who gives to all men liberally and it shall be given him." James 1:5

Our Godly discernment happens in three arenas. The first is in the human experience. Discerning the intent of those that we deal with, either in business or personal life. The second is with evil spirits. We can discern if the circumstance happening to us now in from Satan or just a random occurrence due to natural happenings. Finally, we can discern the Holy Spirit of God as he communicates with us.

The perspective that enables discernment is the belief that God is in control and wants his children to take dominion over the earth and our lives in particular. Our mindset gives us the discernment to make Godly choices.

CHAPTER EIGHT

Perspectives Transform The Mind

Here's how the Bible says we can be transformed. I see it as taking a seven-day journey, walking in the scriptures. You may wish to keep a journal, jotting down your feelings and revelations from God as you move from day to day. Seven steps can make all the difference.

I suggest one day per step to absorb all the Biblical truth in that step. However, one day may not be enough. You may need one week or even more. Take all the time you need. The goal is to get God's Word in you so you can use it. The effort is to establish or re-establish a Godly Mindset that brings about a perspective that is pleasing and acceptable to God. So, let's look at the 1st of 7 steps in renewing your mind.

Step #1... Become A Living Sacrifice

Most of us get up each day running away from life or trying to master it with all our energies. Paul tells us that we are to present ourselves unto God as a, *"Living Sacrifice."* He further says that this action is reasonable considering what Christ did for us. Romans 12:2

Paul's admonition to sacrifice ourselves to God did not mean physical death. Being a sacrifice did not mean being burned on the altar, as the Mosaic Law required, but we're to sacrifice the world we live in with all its evil and to deny ourselves any evil lifestyle associated with it. This is what is meant by a *living* sacrifice. We go on living but not as we did before; in riotous living, drunkenness, immorality, adultery, and all the other deeds of the flesh spoken of in Galatians chapter five.

What does a living sacrifice look like?

The following verse (Romans 12:2) helps us to understand. We become a living sacrifice by not being conformed to this world. The world is defined for us in 1 John 2:15-16 as the lust of the flesh, the lust of the eyes, and the pride of life. All that the world has to offer can be reduced to these three things.

The lust of the flesh includes everything that appeals to our appetites and involves excessive desires for food, drink, sex, and anything else that satisfies physical needs.

Lust of the eyes mostly involves materialism, coveting whatever we see that we don't have and envying those who have what we want.

The pride of life is defined by any ambition for that which puffs us up and puts us on the throne of our own lives.

Our transformation away from this world happens as we renew our minds. We do this primarily through the power of God's Word. The Holy Spirit teaches us as we read the Bible and pray. This is the only power on earth that can transform us from worldliness to true spirituality. As a daily exercise, try giving up all your worldly (evil) desires. This can mean not cursing, not gossiping, not catching an attitude, forgiving others, and so on. Read Galatians chapter five. You will find a list of the deeds of the flesh. Avoid them at all cost.

Sacrificing your will to do the will of God is not easy because you are used to being in charge as your own lord and master. Now, you will have to make Jesus Lord of your life and absolutely surrender to him.

It will also mean that you should employ the fruit of God's Spirit and apply it in all that you do. Again, Galatians chapter 5 will list them. It all happens in prayer where we submit to the revealed will of God and seek earnestly to apply it in our daily actions. The buzz word for step #1 is **Apply! Apply! Apply!**

When you example the deeds of the flesh, you conform to this world.

When you apply or walk in the fruit of God's Holy Spirit, you confirm your Christianity, establish your life's path and destiny.

So, to accomplish step #1, we must identify all that is of this world that offends God and deny it access into our thoughts and lifestyle. Here's what I do…I go to my Heavenly Father in prayer and offer myself to him as an instrument of his good pleasure. I join with my wife in daily prayer, pleading the Blood of Christ over all that we have and are. I give everything I own or will ever have to him, for his glory and I bind Satan and every other evil force away from my dwelling, family and possessions. I do this in the name of Jesus.

Now here comes the hard part. During the day, as evil suggests lustful actions, I fight with all I have, in the name of Jesus, to cast them down and away from me. Then I draw near to God and cry out for help to overcome the inward desires of the flesh and/or the outward temptations that seek to torment me. Sometimes I win. Sometimes I don't. However, when I fail, I know that I have an advocate with my Heavenly Father. That advocate is none other than Jesus, my Lord and Savior. (I John 2:1) He speaks for me before the throne of God and his blood cleanses me from all unrighteousness. (I John 1:9) So I go on sacrificing my inward life of sin, denying it at every turn and receiving the Holy Spirit of promise. I thus become a, "Living Sacrifice". It's working for me and it can also work for you.

Step #2… Change Your Thought Life

After you have mastered being a, "Living Sacrifice", at least trying every day, the next step is to **Change Your Thought Life…**Proverbs 23:7 says, "**For as a man thinketh in his heart, so is he:**" We are what we think.

Have you ever evaluated the thoughts that flow through your mind? I have and I can't keep up with them. They come at me so fast and are like a fleeting image that zips away in a flash, leaving me blessed or cursed as it goes.

What we allow to enter into our minds is the raw material that is used to shape the reality we will experience. Think about it. A man that watches pornographic videos, fills his mind with lustful acts against women. His thought life becomes pornographic and his actions vile and corrupt.

On the other hand, a man that reads his Bible and receives divine revelation from God; fills his mind with truth and is set free from the snares of the devil and the habitual practice of sin.

The apostle John tells us that we will know the truth and it will set us free. The freedom Jesus offers is a *spiritual* freedom from the bondage of sin that is evident in the release from the lifestyle of habitual sin. **John 8:32**

Jesus is the Truth (John 14:6). Knowing the Truth will set you at liberty. You will be free from sin, free from condemnation, and free from death. (Romans 6:22; 8:1–2)

Thought Control

So then…in order to be transformed by the renewing of our minds, we need to control the thoughts that enter into our minds. Can this really be done in a world where almost every TV ad has a sexual overtone and movies are themed in violence? Yes, it can be done but it will take some effort on our part. Listen to Paul again as he writes to the Corinthians…II Corinthians 10:4-6

"For though we walk in the flesh, we do not war after the flesh: For the weapons of our warfare are not carnal, but mighty through God to the pulling down of strong holds; Casting down imaginations, and every high thing that exalts itself against the knowledge of God, and bringing into captivity every thought to the obedience of Christ; And having in a readiness to revenge all disobedience, when your obedience is fulfilled."

Here Are The Key Points To Consider:

1. We must be in obedience to the revealed will of God. That is to say, "Live Up To The Light You Have Been Given"
2. Capture every thought that is against what God has revealed to you. If it goes against the Word of God, bring it into captivity using the knowledge of God. (What you know to be true)
3. Cast it down (Give it no more place in your thought life.)
4. Take upon yourself a tone or attitude of revenge against thoughts that suggest disobedience or lawlessness.

I remember a time when I was backslidden and had drifted away from God. It was a terrible time of sadness and confusion. When I finally heard from my Lord, it was in the spirit and he said, "John? It's a long way back. Are you willing to take the journey?" I immediately said, yes Lord. Then I heard him say again,

"Your heart is like a field that now is full of thorns and weeds. We will have to pull up all the bad stuff and replant good stuff. However, I won't leave you alone. We'll do it together." Jesus and I have been cleaning up my heart ever since and planting the Word of God. As a result of all the effort, my thought life is better and my reality is different. It's better than it was before.

Sources of Thoughts

Believe it or not, all thoughts you think are not your own. I have noticed the following sources of thoughts:

- **The Devil**…he sends, "Fiery Darts" that are meant to pierce our souls and destroy our dreams.
- **God**…who sends us divine revelation, unction and truth that are designed to set us free; direct our paths and encourage us in the faith.
- **People**…Their voices are constantly in our heads as they try to dominate us, sway our judgments, and put us under their pecking order.
- **The, "Old Man"**…We can and do think independently from others. However, the, "Old Man", otherwise known as, "The Flesh" is constantly spreading negative thoughts in front of us.

The negative voices are loud and always say, "You Can't Do It" You're Not Good Enough", etc. So…what are you thinking about? Examine your thoughts; toss out what is wrong or offensive to God and hang on to what God says is good. Hold everything is the light of the knowledge of God (The Bible) and stand in the belief that you are God's child and therefore victorious over sin, death, Satan, hell, bad people, depressing circumstances or whatever.

I look for the source of the thought and then act accordingly. Sometimes the thought will overwhelm you and even torment you before you can figure it out. That's ok because the battle is not over until you fight back and cast it down. The way to win is to make a declaration of faith. Jesus used the scriptures as his declaration of faith when confronted by temptation.

He said things like, Matthew 4:4, **"Man shall not live by bread alone, but by every word that proceeds out of the mouth of God"**. And Luke 4:12,

"And Jesus answering said unto him, It is said, **"Thou shalt not" tempt the Lord thy God"**

Step #2 is an exercise in applying the Word of God to destroy bad thoughts, no matter where they come from. You can measure your day-to-day progress by examining your thoughts. After a while, that which you battle will no longer show up at your door.

The secret is to apply what Paul told the 1st century church. He said, "Finally, brethren, whatsoever things are true, whatsoever things are honest, whatsoever things are just, whatsoever things are pure, whatsoever things are lovely, whatsoever things are of good report; if there be any virtue, and if there be any praise, *think on these things."* Philippians 4:8

Step #3 …Stay In A Continual Attitude of Prayer

We are admonished to, " Pray Without Ceasing." 1 Thessalonians 5:17 No one can pray continually but we can strive to stay in an attitude of conversational prayer, talking to God about our day, our dreams and our destiny. We can even cast our cares upon him because he cares for us and wants to help us to overcome. (I Peter 5:7)

Holy Spirit Interaction

This 3rd step in renewing our minds is to establish a relationship with the Holy Spirit and listen to what he has to say. His participation and your submission are vital to the success of renewal.

Some of my unsaved friends laugh at me when I tell them I talk to God. They jokingly say, "Does he talk back to you?" I tell them, "Yes, he sure does." God has spoken to us through the Bible. He left us over 3,000 promises to dwell on and 66 books written over thousands of years to read and meditate in.

I can surely say that I know God. I saw him first in the scriptures. He is there in full array. You can see his character; feel his compassion; discover his will for your life; and be taught by him personally.

If you question the idea of talking to the Holy Spirit, read what he is doing in your life even now. Instead of denying his presence, reach out to him and strengthen your bond of love with God. Here are a few scriptures to ponder: Listen to what the Bible says about the Holy Spirit's interaction with the child of God.

1. "And I will pray the Father, and he shall give you another Comforter, that he may abide with you forever;" John 14:16
2. "The Spirit itself bears witness with our spirit, that we are the children of God:" Romans 8:15
3. "The Helper, the Holy Spirit, whom the Father will send in my name, will teach you everything and make you remember all that I have told you." (John 14:26)
4. "When they finished praying, the place where they were meeting was shaken. They were all filled with the Holy Spirit and began to proclaim God's message with boldness." (Acts 4:31)
5. "In the same way the Spirit also comes to help us, weak as we are. For we do not know how we ought to pray; the Spirit himself pleads with God for us in groans that words cannot express." (Romans 8:26)
6. "When you heard the message of truth, the gospel of your salvation, and when you believed in him, you were also sealed with the promised Holy Spirit. He is the down payment of our inheritance, for the redemption of the possession, to the praise of his glory." Ephesians 1:13-14
7. "Now there are varieties of gifts, but the same Spirit, and there are varieties of ministries, but the same Lord. There are varieties of results, but it is the same God who produces all the results in everyone. To each person has been given the ability to manifest the Spirit for the common good." I Corinthians 12:1-11
8. "For all who are led by God's Spirit are God's children." Romans 8:14
9. "What? Know? ye not that your body is the temple of the Holy Ghost

which is in you, which ye have of God, and ye are not your own?" 1 Corinthians 6:19

10. "For his Spirit searches out everything and shows us God's deep secrets. No one can know a person's thoughts except that person's own spirit, and no one can know God's thoughts except God's own Spirit. And we have received God's Spirit (not the world's spirit), so we can know the wonderful things God has freely given us. When we tell you these things, we do not use words that come from human wisdom. Instead, we speak words given to us by the Spirit, using the Spirit's words to explain spiritual truths." 1 Corinthians 2:7-13
11. "for the kingdom of God is not eating and drinking, but righteousness, peace, and joy in the Holy Spirit." Romans 14:17
12. "And be not drunk with wine, wherein is excess; but be filled with the Spirit;" Ephesians 5:18

Don't be afraid to talk to the Holy Spirit. He is given to us as a Teacher, Guide, Comforter, Seal of Redemption, and he bears gifts that edify us and bless the body of our Lord, the church.

Stay tuned in and you will hear from God and discover his will for your life. This is the third step in renewing your mind. I call it *"Practicing The Presence of God."* Remember, it's just conversational prayer in which you give God the authority to operate in your life, counsel you and guide you.

Step #4 ...Always Be Thankful

There is too much negativity in this world. It seems, as though life is mostly sad and depressing. I guess that's because of a liberal media that is bent on showing all the bad stuff. You'd think that there is nothing happening that is good. Well, God wants us to see only the good. He wants us to be happy, have life in abundance and to always be thankful. Listen to what the Word of God says on this subject.

"In everything give thanks: for this is the will of God in Christ Jesus concerning you." 1 Thessalonians 5:18

I know that you are questioning this step. How can we give thanks in everything. When things get bad and we suffer, how can we be thankful?

Most folks blame God for bad things that come their way. We should remember that God is a God of Love and has not dealt with us after our own sin. (Psalm 103:10) We are not being punished. You've heard it said that "It rains on the just and the unjust", right?

Hear Peter in I Peter 5:8 "Be sober, be vigilant; because your adversary the devil, as a roaring lion, walketh about, seeking whom he may devour:" The devil is hard at work trying to devour us but in verse nine Peter tells us what to do…" Whom resist steadfast in the faith, knowing that the same afflictions are accomplished in your brethren that are in the world."

Note: He didn't say, "Do battle or make war" He said resist by standing in the faith God has given you.

You should be aware that we are not to give thanks for the thing that is attacking us. (In everything, not for everything) That means we are to look for the good and focus our energies on the blessings of our Lord in that situation. Here's an example…

You get into a car accident. It was not your fault. The car is totaled but you are not hurt, just shaken up a bit. You have two choices.

1. to concentrate on the loss of your car and the stupidity of the other driver and tell everyone you know about your loss. This will gather sympathy and some will even console you.
2. To concentrate on the fact that God kept you safe from harm and you didn't get hurt. This will glorify God in the situation and draw you closer to him as you see his hand in your life.

Now I also know that sometimes things are really hard to deal with and cause much grief like the loss of a loved one, a loss of a good paying job, kids going astray, divorce, etc. Even these hard things to bear have a glimmer of light and hope for the future. Listen again to the scriptures as Paul writes in Romans 8:28-31.

"And we know that all things work together for good to them that love God, to them who are the called according to his purpose. For whom he did foreknow, he also did predestinate to be conformed to the image of his Son, that he might be the firstborn among many brethren. Moreover, whom he did predestinate, them he also called: and whom he called, them he also justified: and whom he justified, them he also glorified. What shall we then say to these things? If God be for us, who can be against us?" Romans 8:28-31

We can still hang on to the fact that we are called according to his purposes, we love God and therefore are assured that all things will work together for our good.

Being thankful and giving thanks to God is a, " MINDSET". We resolve to not blame God; to always see the good and never dwell on the negative. It's hard to get depressed, become angry or dwell in negativity when you are thanking God for every little and big thing. In every situation, we bless God and trust him to work on our behalf.

Step #5...Believe That Every Day Is A New Day

Have you ever encountered a person that lives in the past? They are all around us. They seem to live in the past or in the future but seldom in TODAY. They plan for the future, cry over the past and hide from reality because TODAY is too close and has too many unexpected events that force them to deal now in a confrontational posture.

Hear what the Bible says about TODAY..."*This is the day which the LORD hath made; we will rejoice and be glad in it." Psalm 118:24*

If we believe that every day is the day that the Lord has made, it will be easier to live out that day, knowing he has created it just for us. We can indeed, rejoice and be glad in it.

Hear what the Bible says about God's mercy in every new day... "*God's mercies are "new every morning" (Lamentations 3:23).*

We also now know, without a doubt, that God's mercy, (Unmerited Favor), is new every morning. That means he does not hate us for what went on yesterday. He may be disappointed but we are his children and thus subject to his correction. He leads us to repentance and starts all over again, as if yesterday never happened.

We need to avoid the, **"If Only"** trap. You know what I mean? "if only I'd done better in my marriage" "If only I said no to drugs" "If only"…(you add the thing that you most hate and wish it had never happened.) These things can become strongholds that capture our thoughts, shape our reality and keep us in bondage.

I feel good about TODAY because God made it. Therefore, I can let tomorrow take care of itself and drop yesterday from my thinking. God is not mad at me. His Holy Spirit is with me and will help my infirmities. Romans 8:26)

The above statement reflects the attitude that will transform you as you use it to renew your mind. However, you should be aware of another thing that Paul says about this renewal.

In Ephesians 4:23 Paul uses a striking phrase to parallel Romans 12:2. He says, **"Be renewed in the spirit of your minds."** Now what in the world is that? "The spirit of your mind." It means that the mind has a "spirit." In other words, our mind has what we call a **"mindset."** It doesn't just have a view. It has a viewpoint. It doesn't just have the power to perceive and detect; it also has a posture, a demeanor, a bearing, an attitude, a bent. "Be renewed in the **spirit** of your mind."

Day Five and all days are steps in the renewal process that form a "Mindset" in which we move, live and have our being. The belief that Every Day Is A New Day is part of that mindset. Live in that perspective and you will find God's will and live out his destiny for your life.

God wants us to have his Mind (his thoughts, his viewpoint) in every situation. He wants us to have the supernatural ability to discern everything that happens from His vantage point and his perspective. If we can see from his perspective, we'll be able to "soar" above our circumstances, leaving our problems and trials behind.

Step #6… Guard Your Spirit

In Step #2, I discussed changing your thought life. Now I'd like to further develop that so you have a deeper understanding.

Proverbs 23:7 says, "**For as he thinketh in his heart, so is he:**" We are what we think. Jesus talked about a man that committed adultery because he thought about having a sexual relationship with a woman that was not his.

"But I say unto you, that whosoever looks upon a woman to lust after her hath committed adultery with her already in his heart." (Matthew 5:28) We don't want to fall into this trap.

We need to guard our hearts so those type of feelings do not overwhelm us. They are rooted in lust and will defile us.

It's important to understand that the devil will shoot fiery darts at us that are meant to draw us away from God into our own lustful nature. Sometimes we cannot stop the attack but we can reject its suggestive allure. In other words, we don't have to participate.

Listen to the scriptures..."Watch over your heart with all diligence, for from it flows the springs of life. Put away from you a deceitful mouth, and put devious speech far from you. Let your eyes look directly ahead, and let your gaze be fixed straight in front of you. Watch the path of your feet, and all your ways will be established." – Proverbs 4:23-26 (emphasis added)

Thoughts Cause Feelings that Affect Emotions

We all know that some people are more emotional than others. Some even wear their feelings on their shoulder...they are very sensitive. Others are like a rock, seeming unaffected by life's many trials. Regardless of how we feel, we are all subject to a continual flow of thoughts and we must guard our hearts. It is there that we ponder and evaluate and make decisions that are expressed by our emotions.

What comes out of our hearts is what defiles us:

And he said, "What comes out of a person is what defiles him. For from within, out of the heart of man, come evil thoughts, sexual immorality, theft, murder, adultery, coveting, wickedness, deceit, sensuality, envy, slander, pride, foolishness. All these evil things come from within, and they defile a person." –Mark 7:20-23

If we want to know what is in our hearts, we need only to listen to what is flowing out of our mouths. Curse words, hate, anger, fear and the like are of the flesh. However, they flow out because they are already inside. They come from a fallen nature. We also add to that evil when we accept new destructive thoughts. They are added to what is already there.

On the other hand, if we are filled with God's Spirit, we will experience the fruit of that Spirit and our mouths will flow with expressions of Love, Peace, Joy, Longsuffering, Kindness and the other fruit listed in Galatians chapter five.

We are the channels through which good and evil flow. That's why we are admonished to GUARD our hearts…because the issues of life come forth from what is inside. We can allow evil or good to manifest. This forms the basis of our day.

So…our day-to-day reality is dependent upon what we think and what we allow to be planted in our hearts. My wife has a saying that I like and often repeat. She says, *"Let's not go down that road".* It is mostly used when nerves are frayed and we are on the verge of an argument. I also use it when I find myself thinking things that I shouldn't think. I say, "I am not going there" "Get behind me Satan."

Then I call upon the Lord to deliver me from that temptation. I don't always do the right thing here but I do try my best to apply this truth. I am trying and so can you, even if we fail now and then. We can still get up and try again.

Step # 7…Listen For The Whistle

If you watch football, you'll relate to this. You are watching the game and see a player go off sides. The camera focused on the off-side act and then the referee who immediately blows a loud whistle, points straight at the player and screams out, "Off Sides". That's a good picture of what Paul is saying to the Galatians church. Take a listen…

"And let the peace of God rule in your hearts, to the which also ye are called in one body; and be ye thankful." Colossians 3:15

There will be times that confusion will cloud your thought life and you will not see clearly. It will be hard to know what to do. Using the "Peace of God" as a referee will fix all of that.

If you do not have peace from God about the thoughts that trouble you, toss them out. If you feel only confusion in a situation, do not act. Wait until you have peace before acting. All decisions should be done in the arena of *PEACE* after seeking God for counsel. Always allow the Peace of God to be the referee. The God of Peace will blow a whistle if you are off sides and tell you to get back where you belong.

Peace is a state of tranquility or quietness of spirit that transcends circumstances. The term *peace* is described in Scripture as a gift of the Holy Spirit and is a reflection of his character (1 Thessalonians 5:23; Galatians 6:16; 1 Peter 1:2; Hebrews 13:20).

If we are filled with his Spirit, we will have access to and experience the peace of God. We can rest assured that God will use his peace, as Colossians 3:15 suggests. However, Paul does not say that all this happens without our agreement. God will not violate our free will.

That's why Paul says, "Let" or "allow" because to "let" is to be under submission and in concert with. It takes a simple prayer each day to be filled with the Spirit and in agreement that God's peace will be our "Whistle Blower." Thus, we give the Holy spirit the authority to referee over our lives and alert us when we are off sides.

Jesus said, "Peace I leave with you; my peace I give to you. Not as the world gives do I give to you. Let not your hearts be troubled, neither let them be afraid" (John 14:27). It's ok to let the Holy Spirit be your referee. He won't lead you astray. His job is to bring you into the image of Christ and show you the way to glory so you can walk with dignity and glorify God here on this earth.

Certain attitudes can destroy the peace of God. When we equate trust with the assumption that God will give us whatever we want, we set ourselves up for disappointment. The Bible is filled with examples of the opposite happening to God's people (2 Corinthians 12:7–9; Hebrews 11:13; Psalm 10:1).

Trust means we have set our hearts to believe God, whatever may happen. When we insist on being in control, we sabotage God's desire to let us live in peace. When we choose worry rather than faith, we cannot live in peace.

Jesus warned us often about fear and worry (Matthew 6:34; Luke 12:29; Philippians 4:6). Worry is the enemy of peace. God invites us to cast our cares upon him and then let go of them (1 Peter 5:7). If we listen, we'll hear that whistle blowing and the voice of God telling us to trust in him.

Psalm 91:1 holds the secret to living in the "Peace of God:" "He that dwells in the secret place of the "Most High" shall abide under the shadow of the Almighty. I will say of the LORD, he is my refuge and my fortress: my God; in him will I trust."

That secret place is in the presence of God where we can live in his Spirit. That is where we meet God and have fellowship with him. When we walk in his Spirit, we experience all that God is and adorn his very character.

We actually fulfill his desire to create man is his image and likeness. (Gen.1:26) It is here, under the shadow of his wings, that we can remain peaceful, even when circumstances may not be. When we learn to cry out to him in times of trouble, we find that his peace really does pass all human understanding (Philippians 4:7).

Allowing the Peace of God to be your referee in all decision making will keep you on the right track as you renew your mind.

So, how did you do on your 7-Day journey through the Scriptures? I am trusting the Lord that he will give you all the revelation knowledge necessary to equip you to continue in faith.

We all, sooner or later, will face "The Final Perspective." Most of us do not even think of it until we approach 75-80 years old. It is then that we come to grips with the idea of really dying.

When we are young and even in middle age, we look at death as happening to the other guy. I often said that I will live to be 100 but now that I am in my late 70's I question whether that will happen or not.

I have lived to see my mother, my father, my sister and many of my friends pass on into eternity. I can only hope that their path in life took them into God's eternal grace. I know how they believed and the perspectives they held fast to. This gives me a great deal of comfort. I do believe that they are in the loving arms of Jesus.

But what about me? and what about you? Are we coming to the end of our road? Is our path cluttered with shame and degradation? The apostle Paul said, "I have fought the good fight, I have finished the race, I have kept the faith. Finally, there is laid up for me the crown of righteousness, which the Lord, the righteous Judge, will give to me on that Day, and not to me only but also to all who have loved his appearing." 2 Timothy 4:7-8 NKJV.

I believe that we, you and me, can know, without a shadow of a doubt, that we are on the right path in life. We, like Paul, are running the race and will soon reach the finish line. Let it be, dear God, in honor and with praise on our lips to the glory of Jesus.

News flash! Life does not end for believers in Christ. There is a new perspective that takes over at the point of our passing from this world.

The Bible says, "We are confident, I say, and willing rather to be absent from the body, and to be present with the Lord." 2 Corinthians 5:8

This is a perspective that takes us through death into life eternal. We have this hope in us because "God so loved the world that he sent his only begotten Son, that whosoever believes in him should not perish but have eternal life." John 3:16

When our perspectives are based upon the Word of God, we can rest knowing that God does not lie. Jesus overcame death, hell and the grave. He was resurrected on the 3rd day and ascended into heaven to be seated at the right hand of God, the Father and now intercedes for us who have believed in him.

The new perspective is the promise of God to redeem us and to call us to himself. With that in mind, we have no fear of death. We are in Jesus and he will take us through it on the way to life eternal.

CHAPTER NINE

Perspectives Stand By Faith

I felt it necessary to restate part of what I said in my introduction. It is the perfect segway into this chapter. Here we go...

You'll remember what Jesus said about faith and the mustard seed. "for verily I say unto you, If ye have faith as a grain of mustard seed, ye shall say unto this mountain, Remove hence to yonder place; and it shall remove; and nothing shall be impossible unto you." Matthew 17:20 His perspective was based upon doing the impossible. He actually believed that the impossible was possible if you believed.

His divine perspective or should I say "Point of View" led him to heal the sick, feed the 5,000 from a few loaves of bread and a couple of fish, cast out devils from tormented folks and even raise the dead. His view was not clouded with sin. His Heavenly Father was greater than anything and anyone.

The odd thing about this, "Divine perspective," is that Jesus told his disciples that they could also experience this type of reality. All they had to do is have faith, not a great amount of faith but a small amount, as little as a mustard seed, which is the smallest of all seeds.

The dictionary defines faith this way:

1. complete trust or confidence in someone or something
2. a strong belief in God or in the doctrines of a religion, based on spiritual apprehension rather than proof.
3. a system of religious belief such as: *"the Christian faith"*

4. a strongly held belief or theory:

The Bible, on the other hand expresses faith this way:

"Now faith is the substance of things hoped for, the evidence of things not yet seen" Hebrews 11:1

The "Christian Faith" is a strong belief in a God that you cannot see; that created all things; that sees all things before they happen; that knows the beginning from the end; that is eternal, holy, righteous, loving, full of joy, peace, longsuffering, kindness and has a plan to redeem man from sin and death.

1. Here's what the Bible says about faith:
2. Romans 10:17 - So then faith cometh by hearing, and hearing by the word of God.
3. Hebrews 11:6 - But without faith it is impossible to please him: for he that cometh to God must believe that he is, and that he is a rewarder of them that diligently seek him.
4. Ephesians 2:8-9 - For by grace are ye saved through faith; and that not of yourselves: it is the gift of God: Not of works, lest any man should boast.
5. 2 Corinthians 5:17 - For we walk by faith, not by sight.
6. Romans 1:17 - For therein is the righteousness of God revealed from faith to faith: as it is written, *The just shall live by faith.*
7. Galatians 3:26 - For ye are all the children of God by faith in Christ Jesus.

There are more scriptures about faith but I think these will do for now. The point is that faith is the exercise of your perspective. Your belief is your point of view on a particular subject. When you walk in faith or by faith, you are standing up for what you believe and exercising your God-given right to fellowship with your Heavenly Father in the Spirit and above the sorrow that this world tries to shove down your throats.

When it comes to life, faith is essential. Hear what the Bible says, " I am crucified with Christ: nevertheless I live; yet not I, but Christ lives in me:

and the life which I now live in the flesh, I live by the faith of the Son of God, who loved me, and gave himself for me." Galatians 2:20

Life, for a Christian, is a life of faith but not his or her own. It is the faith of the Son of God that makes life on earth worth living. How do we get that faith? We get the faith of the Son of God, which is Jesus, by being filled with his Spirit. He offers his Spirit to everyone that believes in him. In fact, if you do not have the Spirit dwelling in you, you are not a Christian. Let me show you why.

"In whom ye also trusted, after that ye heard the word of truth, the gospel of your salvation: in whom also after that ye believed, ye were sealed with that holy Spirit of promise," Ephesians 1:13

"For ye have not received the spirit of bondage again to fear; but ye have received the Spirit of adoption, whereby we cry, Abba, Father. The Spirit itself bears witness with our spirit, that we are the children of God:" Romans 8:15-16

When it comes to death, we need not worry. We can trust in Jesus to take us through that door into his glorious kingdom. Here's what the Bible says, "Jesus said unto her, I am the resurrection, and the life: he that believeth in me, though he were dead, yet shall he live: And whosoever lives and believes in me shall never die. Believe thou this?" John 11:25-26

Note: The Biblical meaning of death is eternal separation from God. Physically passing on from this reality is not considered death unless you are not, "Born Again" We never die because, as Paul tells us in II Corinthians, "To be absent from the body is to be present with the Lord.

The phrase "absent from the body" is found in 2 Corinthians 5:6-8. Paul states that he is confident in his eternal destiny and longs for the day when he can be "absent from the body" and be present with the Lord he loves and serves. To be "absent" from one's body simply means to die because, at death, the spirit is separated from the body and moves into its eternal abode either heaven with the Lord or hell, separated from God for eternity.

In the same way, Christians are always confident, knowing that while we are at home in the body, we are absent from the presence of God. For we walk by faith, not by sight. We are confident, yes, well pleased rather to be absent from the body and to be present with the Lord. When a born-again believer dies, his soul goes immediately into the presence of the Lord. There, the soul consciously awaits the resurrection of the body. To the church at Philippi, Paul wrote from a Roman prison (Explanation taken from Gotqueestions.com)

When it comes to daily living, Christ is essential. His wisdom and "Divine Perspective" fit every need and every situation. If Jesus is our Lord, he rules the day, not us. Hear again what Paul said to the Galatians…

" I am crucified with Christ: nevertheless I live; yet not I, but Christ lives in me: and the life which I now live in the flesh, I live by the faith of the Son of God, who loved me, and gave himself for me." Galatians 2:20

The life I now live in the flesh…that is every day stuff, I do not count on myself to rule but see myself crucified with Christ and him on the throne of my life. I live now by his faith not my fears. Galatians 2:20

"And we know that all things work together for good to them that love God, to them who are the called according to *his* purpose. For whom he did foreknow, he also did predestinate *to be* conformed to the image of his Son, that he might be the firstborn among many brethren.

Moreover, whom he did predestinate, them he also called: and whom he called, them he also justified: and whom he justified, them he also glorified. he did predestinate, them he also called: and whom he called, them he also justified: and whom he justified, them he also glorified." Romans 8:28-30

The above scriptures tell us that we are destined to be like Jesus. His divine perspective will be ours when we renew our minds and establish mindsets that keep us filled with the Spirit and strengthens or faith.

CHAPTER TEN

Perspectives And Spiritual Warfare

Our perspectives need to be thought out and examined for any falsehoods or erroneous conclusions. Many a Christian have built their perspectives on half-truths and downright error.

Recently, I have discovered such a situation. There are those in the Christian community that tell us that we are in a continual battle with evil forces and we better have a clear perspective on the subject so we do not fall on the battlefield. I wholeheartedly agree with that view point but I do feel it needs a lot more discussion.

The issue is…do we live under the sovereignty of God, as his children, not really needing to fight the good fight of faith? Or…do we live in a world of sin and rebellion against God that requires us to be on guard all the time to protect ourselves and our families from Satanic attacks? Or…could it be a mix of both blended into a perspective that keeps us in God's eternal blessings?

The Sovereignty theory goes like this:

If we rely completely on the sovereignty of God, we can rest in his divine care. The war is over. God won. Lucifer, the devil or Satan, whoever we want to call him, was cast out of heaven with all his followers. They are now disembodied spirits placed is chains of darkness. Jude 1:6

They will never see the light of God's glory again until the final judgment. Therefore, there is no reason to worry. God is for us and has made provisions for us to be with him. He works all things together for good. Spiritual warfare is no longer needed. The battle is done, won, kaput. We are to live out our lives under God's grace.

On the other hand, if the war is over and Jesus really did totally defeat Satan, which he did:

1. Why does Paul tell us that fiery darts are being tossed at us? *Ephesians 6:16*
2. And why do we need to cast down every imagination and high thought that rises up above the knowledge of God? *II Corinthians 10:4-9*
3. If Satan has no weapons, why is he, as a roaring lion, attacking Christians? *I Peter 5:8-9*
4. Why are we asked to put on the whole armor of God? *Ephesians 6:10-16*
5. Why does Paul tell the church that their weapons are not carnal but mighty to the pulling down of strong holds? 2 Corinthians 10:4-5
6. Why does the Bible say that we wrestle against principalities, against powers, against the rulers of the darkness of this world, against spiritual wickedness in high places? Ephesians 6:12
7. Why does God say" The angel of the LORD encamps round about them that fear (Reverence) him, and delivers them? Psalm 34:7

Here's what I think about all of this:

The battle is over and we won but the war continues. Satan was stripped of any and all power by the finished work of Christ on the cross. Colossians 2:15

But Satan still wages war against the saints. He has no authority or spiritual weapons. He fights with lies, deception and snares, in hopes that he can trick the child of God into doing what he wants, thereby stealing his birthright, i. e. authority and power. John 10:10

His lies have led many an unsuspecting soul down the road to destruction. Did you hear about the teenager that took drugs, just one time, and overdosed? In the hospital, the teen kept saying, "My friends said it was ok and I would feel great."

How about the girl that was told by her health clinic that her pregnancy was just a blob and she could abort it if she didn't want it? She didn't know that a fetus has a heartbeat within 5 ½ to 6-weeks of pregnancy. That's just about the time a girl would notice she is late.

Then there is the guy that realized he could enslave others and sell them to rich buyers, making lots of money.

These are just a few situations that actually happened because certain folks believed a lie and acted on it. They did the bidding of Satan whose goal is to kill, steal and destroy. Satan had no weapons or even an organized army. He uses deception and lies to get human beings to do what he wants.

The Devil's Crowd

It is true that our battle is with demons who are spiritual beings bent on our destruction. However, the devil also works through people. I call them, "The Devil's Crowd" This group consists of folks that deny Jesus as coming in the flesh. They are those that the Bible calls, "anti-Christs." They are "False Prophets" and "False Teachers." They support abortion, same sex marriage, child pornography, wife swapping, human trafficking and all the liberal agenda currently being pushed in our society. They are also in our churches distorting the truth and twisting the words of the Lord to meet their own needs.

Sadly enough, these folks are in many instances, our parents, kids, neighbors, political officials, teachers and co-workers. Satan uses them to spread his "anti-Christ" message.

My wife, just for the fun of it, searched the Internet for crime in our area. She found all sorts of evil going on, all within one mile from our home. Now that's scary. However, Satan will use anyone that is not on guard spiritually to attack God's children. He has a host of demons that do his bidding and they are relentless. However, Jesus defeated all the powers of darkness and gave us his victory. In his name, we can overcome the wiles of the devil.

Satan's army now is the masses of the humanity. The Bible says, "And every spirit that confesses not that Jesus Christ is come in the flesh is not of God: and this is that *spirit* of antichrist, whereof ye have heard that it should come; and even now already is it in the world. I John 4:3

The battle these days is in the mind. We fight off the evil desires of our own hearts as well as the lies and suggestions of spirits that seek our harm. We also face the attitudes and criticism of that spirit of anti-Christ who now operates in the children of disobedience.

It is important that we realize that God is sovereign and he is leading us through this upside-down crazy world. It is also important to see that we are in a life and death struggle with evil. Spiritual warfare is alive and well. However, we are not asked to fight. Instead, we are asked to stand in the armor of our God and resist. The good fight of faith is to resist, holding fast the profession we declared when we were, "Born Again."

"If God be for us, who can be against us?" Romans 8:31 I can see lots of folks, lots of "Who" people that can and are against us. Here's what the Scripture says in Romans 8:30-34

"And those whom he predestined he also called, and those whom he called he also justified, and those whom he justified he also glorified. What then shall we say to these things? *If God is for us, who can be against us?*

He who did not spare his own Son but gave him up for us all, how will he not also with him graciously give us all things? Who shall bring any charge against God's elect? It is God who justifies. Who is to condemn?

Christ Jesus is the one who died—more than that, who was raised—who is at the right hand of God, who indeed is interceding for us."

It is true that we are the righteousness of God in Christ Jesus and therefore blameless in his sight. Here's how it looks in the scriptures:

1. Even the righteousness of God *which is* by faith of Jesus Christ unto all and upon all them that believe: Romans 3:22
2. For therein is the righteousness of God revealed from faith to faith: as it is written, the just shall live by faith. Romans 1:17

3. For he hath made him *to be* sin for us, who knew no sin; that we might be made the righteousness of God in him. 2 Corinthians 5:21

However, that does not exempt us from suffering persecution and demonic attacks. Remember what Jesus said to his disciples? *"Remember the word that I said unto you, The servant is not greater than his lord. If they have persecuted me, they will also persecute you; if they have kept my saying, they will keep yours also."* John 105:20

Who is it then that will come against the children of God? Is it not those that hate Jesus and do not believe in or obey him? The Bible calls these folks anti-Christ. As I said before, they do not believe that the Son of God came in the flesh and is the coming "Christ."

Paul did say that these anti-Christ have already invaded planet earth and dwell among us. They are actively warring against the saints to stop the spread of Christianity and discredit the message of the gospel.

I hold fast to what I have been saying all along. Jesus defeated the powers of darkness and gave us authority over them all so we, in his name, can not only stand against evil trickery, lies and snares but to actually take back what the devil has stolen.

We may not have the ability to rule over the entire earth but we, because of Jesus, can take dominion over our lives and situations that come our way. We can stand against the roaring lion of I Peter 5:8 resisting him in the faith and watch as he flees away in utter defeat.

We can hold up our "Shield of Faith" and see the fiery darts of hell be quenched. We can, as 2 Corinthians 10:4-9 says, "cast down imaginations and every evil thought by bringing them into captivity to the obedience of Christ."

"Nay, in all these things we are more than conquerors through him that loved us." Romans 8:37 We are the children of God whose names are written in the Lamb's Book of Life and joint-heirs with Christ to a glorious destiny. This is the "Divine Perspective."

CONCLUSION

I hope this seven-day journey has helped you to grow in Christ and to actually achieve the transformation that Paul spoke of in Romans 12:2.

I am aware that shifting a paradigm is not easy. Moving from always being negative to positive in attitude is hard to do. Moving from fear and worry to peace is also very difficult. Some who read this book will probably say that…"you just don't understand". My life is too complicated. My past is way too painful. My…Yada! Yada! Yada!

God never said life would be easy. Nevertheless, God wants us to have his "Mindset". If you want his will, you will apply what you have learned in this seven-day journey until it becomes your way of thinking and your perspective. The "Divine Perspective" is to think like God; to see through his eyes; and to have his mind in you.

So, Let's review. How can we be transformed by the renewing of our minds?

1. Become A Living Sacrifice …by not conforming to this world
2. Change Your Thought Life…by casting down imaginations and evil thoughts that seek refuge in your mind.
3. Stay In A Continual Attitude of Prayer…by talking to God about the small things as well as the major ones.
4. Always Be Thankful…in all things, not for all things.
5. Believe That Every Day Is A New Day…because God has created it just for you.
6. Guard Your Spirit…because fiery darts are being tossed your way from evil spirits.

7. Listen For The Whistle…because God's Peace will referee, letting you know if you are off sides.

I see this seven-day journey as stepping stones to your personal freedom in Christ. It can become the foundation upon which you stand.

My goal is to help you to fully realize the potential of actually becoming a, "New Creature" in Christ and thereby fully equipped and ready to do the will of God.

May our Lord bless you and enrich you and fill you with his good grace as you apply these truths.

REST MY CHILD

Rest my child, says the Lord.
Take thy peace and be restored.
I have provided, thy mouth to feed.
From the beginning, I knew your need.

Do not worry, fret or even fear,
For, my child, I am always near
To bless thy soul with love and grace,
To be with thee, face to face.

Come, my child, near to my throne.
Do not allow your faith to roam.
For those who will not believe
Can never find rest in times of need.

My Word shall see you through.
My grace I freely give to you
That you should rest, thy soul to keep,
Forever delivered from unbelief.

Resting in the Lord is the best way to stay happy. However, it requires faith and trust in God that he will be there for you when you need him. It's kind of neat to relax when fear and anxiety are knocking at your door.

ABOUT THE AUTHOR
JOHN MARINELLI

Rev. Marinelli is an ordained minister, He has formed and been pastor of one church in Wisconsin and was the pastor of another in Alabama. He has also been a youth minister and evangelism director over the years.

Rev. Marinelli has authored several other books including: "Original Story Poems", "The Art of Writing Christian Poetry," "Pulpit Poems," "Moonlight & Mistletoe," "The Mysterious Stranger," "With Eagles Wings," "Mysteries & Miracles," "It Came To Pass," Why Do The Righteous Suffer," "Believer's Handbook of battle Strategies." "Hidden In Plain Sight" "The End of The World, From The Beginning, Shadows in the Light of a Pale Moon," "Mister Tugboat" "An Elephant Named Clyde" "Morning Reign" "Times Past But Not Forgotten" "How To Be Happy" and "How To Have A Victorious Christian Life."(www.marinellichristianbooks.com)

John is an accomplished Christian poet. He also dabbles in songwriting, likes to play chess, sings karaoke and goes fishing now and then. He lives in north central Florida where he enjoys a retired lifestyle with his wife and two collies.

GALLERY OF ENCOURAGING CHRISTIAN POEMS

AGREEING WITH GOD

We speak of things that are not,
Believing in them as though they were,
Because our Heavenly Father spoke them first,
Sending them to us in promises that never blur.

We take Him at His Word,
And listen to all He has to say.
We wrap each promise around our souls,
Until what was spoken becomes our day.

We will agree with the Lord,
Trusting that He knows best.
For only His awesome power,
Can provide our souls with rest.

"As it is written, I have made thee a father of many nations, before Him who he believed, even God who quickens the dead and calls those things that be not as though they were" Romans 4:17

Like Abraham, we also have a destiny that God has spoken into our lives. He calls it forth before it exists. Like Abraham, we are to believe, even against hope, that what God said will indeed come to be. (Romans 4:18).

ARM'S LENGTH

I hold the world at arm's length,
That its choices do not interfere.
While it does its own thing,
I watch and wait over here.

My steps must not go that way,
For it's not where I need to be.
The Lord has shown me the path,
That will lead me to my destiny.

The call of the world is strong
And pulls at me now and then.
But I know that way
Is full of sorrow and sin.

I must move on in life
Beyond their beckoning call.
It's the right thing to do,
So I do not stumble or fall.

I will not be swayed or misled
By family, friends or business deal.
Their secret thoughts are not mine,
To consider, to admire or feel.

So I keep the world at "Arm's Length"
As I journey through this life.
My faith in Jesus keeps me strong,
As I walk in His glorious light.

"Love not the world, neither the things that are in the world. If any man loves the world, the love of the Father is not in him. For all that is in the world, the lust of the flesh, the lust of the eyes and the pride of life, is not of the Father, but of the world. And the world passes away and the lust thereof: But he that doeth the will of God abides forever. I John 2:15-17

It is more important to know God and to follow after Him, than to become entangled in life's lustful traps: for if we were to gain the whole world and lose our own soul, how terrible would that be?

DON'T WORRY

Don't worry about tomorrow.
You did that yesterday.
Go on with your life
And remember always to pray.

Ask and it shall be given to you,
But this great truth you already know.
Rejoice and be happy, why? Because…
Your harvest comes from what you sow.

I will say it again and even more,
Until it becomes very very clear.
Tomorrow will take care of itself,
But worry is another word for fear.

Now here's what I want you to do.
Trust in the Lord and be of good cheer.
Drop the worry from your vocabulary
And cast out that demon of fear.

Worry is the flipside of faith. If you are walking in faith, you are free from worry. Why, because faith hopes in God and trusts that he will be there to meet your need.

TWO HOUSES

We built our homes together,
Mine upon a Rock and his in the sand.
He thought his would be all right,
But he was a foolish man.

God's wisdom showed me the way.
And what I needed to do,
But my foolish neighbor,
Never had a clue.

Then the rains came,
And the winds began to blow.
The storms beat upon our homes,
And we had nowhere to go.

We built our homes together,
My neighbor and me.
Mine is still there upon the Rock,
But his ceased to be.

Wise men and fools both suffer,
The storms that befall mankind.
But those who trust in Jesus
Will always stand the test of time.

Foundation is everything. If you build your life on the Word of God, it will last forever. That's why we strive to be obedient to the will of God. We want his destine and his blessings, no matter what the world system thinks or does.

CLUTTER

Clutter keeps the mind confused,
As images dance through the night.
Lost among those unimportant thoughts,
Are the dreams that once shined bright.

An endless parade of fear and doubt,
Crowds the mind to destroy our day.
Ever soaring on the wings of the soul,
Until it has formed an evil array.

But clutter is by one's choice,
Of those who dance to its beat.
Better to face imaginations' due
Than to fall into utter defeat.

Be Quiet!!! Is our spirit's desperate cry,
As we call upon the name of the Lord.
Silence is our heart's desired prayer,
Until our minds are again restored.

"Keep thy heart with all diligence: for out of it are the issues of life" Proverbs 4:23

We make the final choices in life that either lead us astray or closer to the Lord. We chose what enters our hearts and fills our minds. May we always choose the path of righteousness and the way of peace.

THE LORD'S LITTLE TWO BY FOUR

God has a little 2' X 4'
That rest on heaven's windowsill.
He uses it now and then,
When we stray from His will.

Sometimes we need a good "Bap";
With the Lord's little 2' X 4'
To knock out the confusion,
And help us to desire Him more.

The Lord's little 2' X 4'
Is what we sometimes need,
To get our thinking straight,
And keep our focus indeed.

The Lord's little 2' X 4'
Is fashioned from life's every trial,
So we do not stray from His will,
Or fall into an ungodly lifestyle.

"My son, despise not the chastening of the Lord; neither be weary of His correction: for whom the Lord loves, He corrects; even as a father his son, in whom he delights." Proverbs 3:11 & 12

It is a good thing to be corrected by God. We should not fear His rebuke for it is not His wrath, but rather a blessing from His love that keeps us moving on towards maturity.

I FIND MYSELF IN GOD

I find myself in God.
He is my, "Everything"
I know that He is Lord,
My Life, My Hope, My King.

I find myself in God,
Not the ways of Sin.
Nor do I look to others,
To know who I really am.

I find myself in God,
To whom I bow on bended knee.
He alone is my joy and strength
And where I want to be.

"For we are His workmanship, created in Christ Jesus unto good works, which God hath before ordained, that we should walk in them" Ephesians 2:10

Knowing that we are created in Christ Jesus gives us confidence to walk in Christ, as He walked, along a pathway of good works. It is our joy and pleasure to be like Him. In Him we move and live and have our being.

"I AM" THERE

"I AM" There,
At the end of your broken dreams,
Before the sun rises over your day,
Prior to those tear-filled streams.

"I AM" There,
Down that road of despair,
When all appears to be lost,
And no one seems to care.

"I AM" There,
Over all of life's twists and turns,
When tomorrow is all but gone,
And when you are full of concerns.

"I AM" There,
Sayeth the Lord of Host,
To bring you hope and peace,
And the power of My Holy Ghost.

"I AM" There,
To be sure you make it through,
In the midst of every trial,
To bless your life and deliver you.

"I Am" There

"All power is given unto me in heaven and earth. Go ye therefore and teach all nations, baptizing them in the name of the Father, and of the Son, and of the Holy Ghost: Teaching them to observe all things, whatsoever I have commanded you: and lo, I am with you always, even unto the end of the world." Mathew 28:18-20

The Lord is with us always. He never leaves our side, even when we leave His. In every situation, He is there. It's time to count on His presence and trust in His care.

SO LISTEN UP

I write this verse that all should know.
What I have to say is like a seed, ready to grow.
So listen up to all I have to say.
It could be the very blessing your heart needs today.

God has not given you a spirit of fear.
Instead, He has offered to dry up every tear.
He really loves you, even though you often fail.
His love and mercy follows you,
Enabling you to be the head and not the tail.
So do not worry or even fret.
That's why Jesus paid sin's awful debt.
Now go on in life to discover its victory
Knowing that Jesus has indeed set you free.

"For God hath not given us the spirit of fear: but of Power and of Love and a sound mine" II Timothy 1:7

There is nothing to fear except fear itself and that spirit has been defeated on the cross. We now have the Spirit of power and love and a sound mind. He will never leave us or forsake us. We are truly free.

WINNING THE BATTLE

We must use the Word of God
To calm emotions that fray.
For the enemy never sleeps,
Until he has led us astray.

So when your emotions overflow
With feelings like depression and fear.
Know this! If you dwell in that place,
You invite the enemy to draw near.

When your emotions rage
With fiery darts aglow,
Stand in the power of the Lord,
Against its awful woe.

And if you get confused
And lost in the storm,
Put your thoughts on trial,
Rejecting all but heaven born.

You can win the battle
That rages within your soul.
By casting down imaginations,
And breaking Satan's hold.

Remember to focus on Jesus,
Holding the world at arm's length.
Lift up your head above the trial,
And the Lord will give you strength.

"For the weapons of our warfare are not carnal but mighty, through God, to the pulling down of strongholds: casting down imaginations and every high thing that exalts itself against the knowledge of God, and bringing into captivity every thought to the obedience of Christ." II Corinthians 10:3-5 The battle is in our minds and we win by putting our thoughts on trial and casting out all that oppose the knowledge of God. This is true victory.

THE LIGHTHOUSE

A lighthouse is a blessing,
To the ships that toss in the sea.
For it shows them the way,
Until they can clearly see.

The rage of an angry storm,
Cannot hide its brilliant light.
Nor can its awesome furry,
Rule as an endless night.

Jesus is the lighthouse,
For those who have gone astray.
The light of His love,
Offers a new and living way.
Jesus is the lighthouse,
When fear and sickness rage.
The light of His love,
Gives hope in difficult days.

So trust in the Lord,
And look for His light.
He alone is "The Lighthouse",
That guides you through the night.

"I am the Way, the Truth, and the Life. No man cometh to the Father but by me" John 14:6

Life holds many dark nights that are full of unexpected storms. Only a deep abiding faith in Jesus Christ will get us through. He is the light of the world. His light keeps us from falling into confusion, sorrow, sickness and demonic oppression.

THE WAY MAKER

Only Jesus can make a way,
Through the difficulties of life.
He alone is Lord and King,
Over life's sorrows and strife.

He is the "Way Maker,"
When there is no visible way.
He will make the way known,
As though it were the light of day.

He will make a way,
For those of humble heart.
He will clear away the rubble,
Restoring what Satan broke apart.
Jesus is the "Way Maker,"
A friend to all who are lost.
He has made the way,
Paying sin's incredible cost.

The way to the Maker,
Is through His only Son.
He alone is the "Way Maker,"
Until life's battles are won.

"Let not your heart be troubled. Ye believe in God, believe also in me. In my father's house are many mansions: If it were not so, I would have told you. I go to prepare a place for you. And if I go and prepare a place for you, I will come again, and receive you unto myself, that where I am, there ye may be also." John 14: 1-3

The Lord is prepared for any emergency. He knows the beginning from the end and has gone before us to prepare a way that we can follow until we see Him face to face.

STINKING THINKING

Stinking thinking, they say,
Is bad for your health.
For it frustrates life's goals,
And denies happiness and wealth.

A right perspective is important,
As we think about everything.
It will either bring us down,
Or cause us to shout and sing.

What we think about these days,
Really does affect our life.
It can cause us to overflow with Joy,
Or fall into depression and strife.

So don't let your thinking,
Stink all the way up to heaven.
Stand in faith before God,
And get rid of that negative leaven.

"Then Jesus said unto them, take heed and beware of the leaven of the Pharisees and the Sadducees" Mathew 16:6

Someone once said, "We are what we think" The Bible says, "As a man thinks, so is he" It is important to concentrate our thinking of those things that are of good report, pure, honest and that will keep us clean of heart.

WISE MEN STILL SEEK HIM

Wise men still seek Him
Who appeared so long ago.
They come now by grace
Through faithful hearts aglow.

Wise men still seek Him
For He is their "Bread of Life."
A sustaining inner strength
Through times of sorrow or strife.

Wise men still seek Him
The Christ of Calvary.
God's only begotten Son
Crucified as Sin's penalty.

Wise men still seek Him
Jesus, God in human array.
King of kings & Lord of lords
Born to earth on Christmas Day.

"Now when Jesus was born in Bethlehem of Judea in the days of Herod the king, behold, there came wise men from the east to Jerusalem, saying, where is he that is born king of the Jews? For we have seen his star in the east and are come to worship him" Mathew 2:1-2

Seeking Jesus is the wisest thing any man, woman or child can do and when we find Him, it is our privilege to bow down and worship Him. This is our journey, our destiny and our life while on this earth.

THE ANGELS CRY HOLY

The Angels cry "Holy,"
While sorrow fills the land.
For God's Judgment Day,
Is to come upon every man.

The Angels cry "Holy,"
While mankind goes astray,
Rejecting the love of God,
To follow his own precarious way.

The Angels cry "Holy,"
Knowing the terror of the Lord,
When all who dwell in sin,
Will suddenly be destroyed.

The Angels cry "Holy,"
Waiting for all things new,
Born of the Holy Spirit,
When God's Judgment is through.

The Angels cry "Holy,"
"Holy is the Lamb,"
Waiting for the children of God,
To join "The Great I AM"

"And one cried unto another and said, "Holy, Holy, Holy, is the Lord of host: the whole earth is full of his glory" Isaiah 6:3

We serve a Holy God that deserves our reverence and homage. The angels know this and worship Him, but man, because of sin, has no real concept of his own creator.

A HIGHWAY CALLED "HOLINESS"

He places my feet on
A highway called "Holiness,"
That led my soul
To the throne of God.

Amidst the cheers of angels,
I walk, wearing His holy gown.
Onward towards heaven's throne,
While evil cast its awful frown.

My eyes were opened
That I might see.
Both the good and the evil,
That sought after me.

I walk the highway-Holiness
That crosses all of time.
Towards the throne of God,
Leaving this world behind.

"And an highway shall be there, and a way, and it shall be called, the way of holiness; the unclean shall not pass over it; but it shall be for those: the wayfaring men, though fools, shall not err therein. No lion shall be there, nor any ravenous beast shall go up thereon, it shall not be found there, but the redeemed shall walk there. And the redeemed of the Lord shall return, and come to Zion with songs and everlasting joy upon their heads: They shall obtain joy and gladness, and sorrow and sighing shall flee away. " Isaiah 35:8-10

What a privilege to walk the highway of Holiness. It is prepared especially for us, the redeemed, and it is protected from the errors of fools and the snarl of beast and especially the roar of the lion.

CALL UPON THE LORD

When your burdens overwhelm you,
Like a mighty raging sea.
Call upon the Lord, Jesus,
And He will set you free

When your heartaches are many,
And life is difficult to understand.
Call upon the Lord, Jesus.
He will come and hold your hand.

When your friends reject you,
Because you follow after Him,
Call upon the Lord, Jesus.
And keep yourself from sin.

When you fall into depression,
As though it were a giant pit.
Call upon the Lord, Jesus,
Who will restore your joyful wit.

When you're saddened by the day
Feeling lost and all alone.
Call upon the Lord, Jesus,
Who will make His way known.

When you are weary and heavy laden,
Tired from life's many tests.
Call upon the Lord, Jesus,
Who is sure to give you rest.

"Hear my cry; oh God, attend unto my prayer. From the end of the earth,

I will cry unto thee, when my heart is overwhelmed: Lead me to the rock that is higher than I." Psalms 61:1-2

Calling upon the Lord in stressful times is o.k. He wants us to cry to Him and then to trust in Him to watch over His Word to perform it on our behalf.

IT CAME TO PASS

Things often come to pass,
But seldom do they ever last.
They come into our busy day,
For awhile, then pass away.

We hear their voices, loud and clear,
As they arrive and while they are here.
They speak both joy and misery,
Some to you and some to me.

We say, "It came to pass,"
Or say, "It happened so fast."
Down life's beaten path,
Comes both love and wrath.

So say goodbye to sad and blue.
To all that is now troubling you.
For things will come, only to pass,
But God's love will always last.

"And it came to pass in those days…" Luke2:1

These are the times of our lives. We live them, some for good and some for not so good. One thing is for sure, that which comes our way, comes only to pass on by. It is not what happens that is so important, but rather what we do with what we are faced with.

Trusting in the Lord and seeking His guidance will always conquer that which comes to pass.

THE WHOSOEVER SCENARIO

The "Whosoever" is who so ever,
Not who so won't, can't or will not.
The story is as clear as a sunny day.
God offers a new and living way.

But only those who engage "free will"
To choose life, faith and obedience,
Will find salvation for their souls,
And be cleansed and made whole.

We do the choosing: to accept or deny.
That is how God set it up to be.
He made the call to life's "Whosoever",
That they could live abundantly.

"For God so loved the world, that he gave his only begotten son, that whosoever believeth in him, should not perish but have everlasting life." John 3:16

We are the "Whosoever" in John 3:16, that one day put his or her faith in Christ, believed in Him and now rest in the Lord's love and grace. We have the promise of God that He sent His Son so we could believe and have everlasting life. How great is that?

LITTLE PRISONS

Little prisons await the man with a lustful soul.
Bars of selfishness and pride create dungeons of icy cold.

Prisons of shame and jealousy fill the heart with utter despair.
Bars that separate from God and those that really care.

Stand back! While the doors are tightly closed;
Taking away your life, to wither as a dying rose.

Beware of those little prisons that trap the lustful soul.
Keep yourself free from sin through faith in the Christ of old.

Little prisons need not to be your fate.
It is your choice, Spirit or flesh to date.

"O Foolish Galatians, who hath bewitched you, that ye should not obey the truth, before whose eyes Jesus Christ hath been, evidently set forth, crucified among you? Are you so foolish? Having begun in the Spirit, are you now made perfect in the flesh?

We should always seek to dwell in the Spirit, that we would not emulate the deeds of the flesh. When we fall short, we create "little prisons" that keep us in confusion and away from the blessing of God. It's time to walk in the Spirit and break the prisons that so easily beset us.

A WHISPER IN THE WIND

There's a whisper in the wind
That lingers both day and night.
A champion of truth and justice,
By the power of His might.

A word in due season
That echoes from deep within.
A voice out of nowhere,
Reproving the world of sin.

Look there, in the street
And here, by the shores of the sea.
There's a whisper hidden in the wind;
A voice from eternity.

There's a calling from God.
His voice is hidden in the wind.
In a whisper, He speaks to our hearts
With the love and counsel of a friend.

Listen for the Whisper,
All who seek to know.
It is God's Holy Spirit
Telling you which way to go.

"And thine ears shall hear a word behind thee saying, This is the way, walk ye in it, when ye turn to the right hand and when ye turn to the left" Isaiah 30:21

The voice of the Lord is often a still small voice, yet always clear and it never brings confusion. His voice is like a whisper in the wind that brings a peaceful breeze to the heart. The joy of hearing His voice is to know His will and our destiny.

FRAGILE FLOWER RED

As a flower in earthen sod,
I bloom for thee, oh God.
To blossom with the turn of spring;
To be to you, a beautiful thing.

I lift my Fragile Flower Red
Upward from my earthen bed;
To draw light from God above,
Strength and peace and joy and love.

As a flower, I bloom for thee
That passersby may stop and see.
Your fragrance and beauty I am,
Flowered in grace as a man.

As a flower in earthen sod,
I bloom for thee, oh God.
Upward, I lift my head,
As a Fragile Flower Red.

"Be not conformed to this world, but be ye transformed, by the renewing of your mind, that ye may prove what is that good and acceptable and perfect will of God."

When we look to God as our source, we blossom, much like a flower that draws light from the sun. When we blossom, like a flower, we display the glory and beauty of our creator to all who care to stop and look. This is our divine destiny.

Other books by John Marinelli can be viewed and purchased at: www.marinellichristianbooks.com

www.ingramcontent.com/pod-product-compliance
Lightning Source LLC
Chambersburg PA
CBHW020429010526
44118CB00010B/492